Valentin Fedorov

BORIS YELTSIN
A Political Portrait

Valentin Fedorov is sitting to the right of President Boris Yeltsin in the photograph. Valentin Fedorov is the former Governor of Sakhalin Island, Russia. He is also a professor of economics, and a well-known political figure in Russia. He has written this book about Yeltsin's role in determining the fate of Russia. This book is based on Valentin Fedorov's personal impressions and analysis of the behavior of the top levels of the Russian government.

Through this book, Valentin Fedorov provides the reader with an opportunity to really understand from a Russian's point of view, the struggle the Russian people and government have been through over the past few years.

In editing and translating this book from the Russian language to the English language for publication, Imperial Publishing Company, as much as possible through the translation, reflects the writing style, tone, and intent of Valentin Fedorov. Imperial Publishing Company's intention was not only to convey the thoughts of the author, but also to reflect the language currently in use in Russia today.

Imperial Publishing Company

IVAN

There is no stronger shoulder than his,
In everyday life he wouldn't hurt a fly.
But consumed with firewater
He could put you to death not knowing
his own strength.

He won't hold a grudge.
He enjoys dancing to accordion music.
He likes to play dominoes
And he eats potatoes with his bread.

He is not happy at all
With discord in the Slavic world
And to hold the world at the Kalashnikov
aim,
The border sealed.

On his way to history
He can not trespass
Against repeated adversities
As other nations have.

Valentin P. Fedorov
(Of Sakhalin Island)

YELTSIN
A Political Portrait

Imperial Publishing Company

YELTSIN: A Political Portrait
Imperial Publishing Company / June 1996

Fedorov, Valentin P., 1996

ISBN : 0-9653218-8-6
Library of Congress Number: 96-77425

How To Order:

Single copies may be ordered from Imperial
Publishing Company, 7683 SE 27th Street, Mercer
Island, WA 98040. Phone: (206) 263-2052, Fax:
(206) 236-1915. Quantity discounts are available.

Internet Address: http://www.imperialpublishing.com

Published in the United States

Imperial Publishing Company

PRINTED IN THE UNITED STATES OF AMERICA

The author wishes to thank
the Sakhalin Island Company,
"Tunaycha," and Anatoly I. Filippov,
its President, for their assistance in
publishing this book.

Table of Contents

> *Only the horse knows the burden of the saddle.*
>
> *A Bulgarian saying*

Preface

It so happened that this book emerged on its own, so to speak, without a preconceived plan to write it. In it are my impressions of Boris N. Yeltsin from the very beginning of his political revolt against the previous system to the present. History is not anonymous; its heroes and victims live in our midst, and some of us possibly are among the latter. In this book, the meaning of the events of the past few years are revealed through a study of Yeltsin.

To write about a president who is still in office is not an easy task, and it carries with it a heavy responsibility, particularly if what is written is not of an entirely complimentary nature.

The first two published Russian editions of this work received a variety of reviews. Some readers accused me of partisanship to Yeltsin, while others found me to be an overly harsh critic. This is understandable, since Yeltsin, himself, presents contrary views of himself to the public.

What I have attempted to do here is to look at this man as one should —"with neither hatred nor partiality" (Tacitus).

Russia, a country which for centuries has been a leading world power, is now experiencing a profound crisis, and its people are suffering unjustifiable privations. Russia's primordial regions, from her western borders to Siberia and the Far East, have been driven to decay. Russia has saved many people from the threat of an unsheathed sword. She has selflessly shared with them her natural wealth, despite her own needs. But now she is being subjected to unsubstantiated accusations from some of the former republics of the USSR.

A necessary prerequisite to the restoration of Russia's grandeur is the creation of a new system. A true multi-sectored structure must be created in the economy, along with competition for various types of property ownership. The right of any type of property ownership to exist should be determined not by ideology, but by its effectiveness. In the USSR, economic policies did not serve the people. They were designed to serve an abstract notion, that turned out to be erroneous. No one—no leader, no individual group, no political party, not even the army—can be wiser and more powerful than the people. No one has the right to dictate his will on the people or force messianic plans upon them. Treating the people as the object rather than the subject of the action had dire consequences for post-revolutionary Russia.

The country has been seriously damaged since 1917. One of the chief accusations that must be made about the regime that was established at that time is that it did not allow Russia to assume a leading role in the world economy and, consequently, in world politics. The grandeur of the Soviet Union was built on pure force, without an underlying healthy economic base.

The planning and distribution system could not exist on its own due to the inherent inefficiencies of production; hence, it was propped up by the rapacious exploitation of natural resources. But even natural resources are not limitless. Their depletion and cumulative ecological damage have not only reduced economic growth, but have affected the very quality of life. This has resulted in a significant drop in average life expectancy, an increase in the mortality rate, a decline in public health, and much more.

More and more countries are surpassing Russia in economic development. Establishing a market economy will allow the country to move out from the sidelines into the mainstream of world progress.

There is no doubt that we must move toward a market economy. It is not the market economy itself that is frightening; it is the transition to it. Therefore, the methods of this transition must be changed. We no longer can afford to make mistakes. We just do not have any time.

In June of 1990, leadership changes resulted in a new political direction. Boris N. Yeltsin was elected Chairman of the Supreme Soviet of the RSFSR [the Russian Soviet Federated Socialist Republic]. Much was accomplished during that period. However, fundamental miscalculations were made in the course of reorganization.

The reforms in Russia began while it was still part of the USSR, and assumed massive proportions in 1992 on a platform of a rapid and determined transition to a market economy.

The results of these changes to the economy must be evaluated as being unacceptable and negative. Since 1990, the gross national product has decreased twofold. Half of this decrease stemmed from the breakdown of economic relations after the collapse of the USSR. The Soviet Union's departure from the world stage was such a tremendous event that the severance of economic ties among its parts might be viewed as an objective event caused by anomalous forces. But this is not so. There are specific people who historically (at the very least) are responsible for the demise of the USSR. Those who believe that nothing could have been done to prevent the USSR from collapsing cannot deny another fact: nothing was done in the process of the collapse to recognize and safeguard the interests of Russia. It is Russia that has suffered unjustifiable territorial and economic losses as a result of the dissolving of the USSR. For instance, it lost massive territories that for centuries had been part of Russia—territories that had nothing to do with October 1917, or with the formation of the USSR.

It is no longer possible to blame the decline in productivity on the collapse of the USSR. Since then, a lot of water has gone under the bridge while no serious measures have been taken to create a new foundation for the economy. Worst of all, investments have dropped more than three times since 1990. We are robbing Russia of its industrial future.

Boris N. Yeltsin has left a decisive mark on all the events that took place in the USSR and in Russia since 1990.

The rest of the politicians, from both the supporting and opposing camps, make up the milieu in which he acts. Some are supporters, some are irritants, and others are sparring partners. All of them, however, are lightweights in comparison to him. Books will be written about Yeltsin, whereas the political figures surrounding him may not merit even a full-fledged article, despite the fact that many of them are professors and published authors. Fame is truly defined not by whether you write, but by whether you are written about. When our grandchildren study our times in school, they will see two consecutive names: Gorbachev and Yeltsin. Incidentally, they both react contemptuously to one another. The former because of an understandably uncomfortable feeling toward a successful rival, and the latter for an equally understandable reason: an old resentment of humiliation and suffering that still exists. They can talk about each other end-

lessly, quite naturally omitting rapturous epithets. Be
that as it may, these two men have become a part of history. Their names will be paired as were the names
of Marx and Engels and Lenin and Stalin. The fact
that we, their contemporaries, know them personally
to be worthy men, not affected by the taint of corruption nor choked with a burning desire to have
revenge on their opponents, create traps or demand
blood, should evoke some satisfaction.

It so happened that my first article about Yeltsin
appeared in the magazine "Rodina" [Motherland] in
1990 (issue No. 1) under the title "Politicians Should
Be Predictable." It was printed under the heading, "An
Opposing Opinion." This heading was the invention
of the editorial staff. U. Makartsev, a journalist working for "Rodina," decided to conduct a series of interviews with famous public figures and then invite their
opponents to express their point of view. He offered
me the opportunity to express an opinion of Yeltsin.

Makartsev's interview with Yeltsin took place on
October 19, 1989, at the Moscow Hotel. Some problems arose after its publication along with my commentary. The Central Committee of the Communist
Party voiced objections. Yeltsin was out of favor at
the time and, if his name did surface in the media, it
almost always was the subject of criticism. The official
press did not approve of Yeltsin (and at that time all of
the press was official), but he had already gained pop-

ularity among the people. He was held in good esteem, and pro-Yeltsin flyers as well as writings (sometimes called by their foreign name, "graffiti") appeared on the walls of houses, fences, and bus stops. I would study these expressions of pro-Yeltsin sentiment on my way home from my professor position at the Plekhanov Institute of Agriculture in Moscow. They included both clever and naive notions. For example: "Citizens, at the meeting, Yeltsin promised, if elected, to eliminate all privileges for members of the nomenclature. But not immediately—his wife couldn't take it." Some of the statements were written in verse. This one comes to mind: "Perestoika's not worth a cent without Yeltsin in parliament." The authorities, however, were not at all eager to spread information about Yeltsin that did not compromise him or showed him in a realistic light. A number of periodicals suppressed interviews that were ready for print. "Do you think they will let you print this?" Yeltsin asked Makartsev as he authorized the release of the interview.

The policy of the functionaries in the Central Committee against printed matter was defeated. Published after a two month delay, my article became one of the first sources from which one could learn something about Yeltsin. Following is the article in its entirety, just as I submitted it to the editor of "Rodina" in October of 1989.

Politicians Should Be Predictable

During the many years that I worked in West Germany for the Academy of Sciences of the USSR, I spent several days in the Bundestag and observed the country's legislative body at work by watching television in the comfort of my own living room. Debates among the deputies were par for the course, and a unanimous vote was a rare exception. When, in contrast to this, they showed televised sessions of the Supreme Soviet of the RSFSR with a single burst of hands shooting up, the West Germans would sneer, "It used to be the same here during the Third Reich."

In the West, the parliamentary mechanism has been meticulously polished over the centuries. It rejects the weak and makes way for the capable. There is a well-known, wise saying: "If this system is bad, then the rest are even worse." Thanks to their ever-present competitiveness, the best defenders of the existing order (which, as we now admit, justifies itself in many ways) usually are at the head of the state.

Perestroika changed our political atmosphere beyond recognition, and now our ways of governing and making responsible decisions are allowing us to gradually become part of the civilized world and one of the most visible figures in the upper echelons of our government today is Boris Yeltsin.

His climb up the party hierarchy all the way to the

Politburo (as a Candidate) did not attract much attention at first. He was a new face, but at the same time appeared to be the stereotypical image of a politician. Yeltsin's rebellion in the "Party Olympus" forced people to take notice of this outstanding person. And the fact that the system rejected him resulted in a tremendous (to this day) success for him.

Perestroika changed our political atmosphere to a point beyond recognition, and our new methods of governing and making responsible decisions are slowly making us a part of the civilized world. And one of the most visible figures in the upper echelons of our government today is Boris Nikolaevich Yeltsin.

The phenomenon of Yeltsin that has become (possibly forever) a part of the history of our country can be explained, in my opinion, in the first place, by his personal characteristics. First and foremost is his readiness to sacrifice himself. Of course, during his days as a Moscow party leader, he could not have been ignorant of the fact that by coming out against his powerful colleagues he was committing political suicide, according to the canons of the time. In terms of personal safety, I do not believe he was threatened. But he had to come to terms with the inevitable loss of many privileges. It is not surprising that, among the intelligentsia, similar to the saying, "to live like a king" arose the saying, "to live like a member of the Politburo. " (Incidentally, the former members still live quite well).

Yeltsin consciously rejected material privileges which the average Soviet citizen could not even imagine when he mounted the platform at the October, 1987 plenary session of the CC CPSU [Central Committee of the Communist Party of the Soviet Union]. Later, he lost the privileges. As far as his daily life was concerned, it was an act of material self-deprivation, which could not help but generate deep respect and sympathy. The latter attitude greatly increased after he protested against the illegal privileges of the power elite. Relative to this, I must note, however, that the prime virtue expected of those vested with power is not asceticism or self-imposed discipline in consumption, but rather noble ideas and the wise navigation of the ship of state. I remember when Carter became President of the United States. He went to the White House on foot to demonstrate his economic policies. Nonetheless, in four years, the voters asked him to step down, due to his little-understood policies. The subsequent two terms of President Reagan demonstrated a different set of priorities.

Yeltsin's combative spirit is also impressive. He did not listen to his inner voice (which, as with all of us, constantly torments the soul and frequently wins). He did not give in or break. He stood firm. All alone, without support, he appealed, not to the people (at that time it was not yet acceptable), but to political leaders of various rank. But, clinging to their own positions, they condemned him. It is only now that Yeltsin has supporters. Possibly we will learn in more detail what it must have been like to beat his head against the stone wall of the System as a "one-man team," when we read his memoirs which he is currently putting on tape. This man paid a high price in all respects for his popularity, and if there are those who are envious of him, let them keep this in mind.

In the second place, Yeltsin's unprecedented return as a major political figure was due possibly to the radical social and political changes taking place at the time. Had Yeltsin's enlightened diatribe against the establishment occurred not in 1987, but a few years earlier, his light would have been extinguished in an hour's time. He would have ended up at some low-level agricultural post, far from the capital. Objectionable or failed politicians in our country were punished by being transferred back to where they came from, or were sent as ambassadors to other countries, even if they didn't know the difference between Austria and Australia.

Those in power unwittingly increased Yeltsin's popularity by using less than ethical methods of dealing with him in plain view of the people. Although those in power could no longer use the former methods of reprisal, they were not yet used to the new standards of political life and continued in their attempts to compromise their accuser. But they were not able to do this skillfully—they bungled the job and actually created a martyr. The powers that we must remember are that in Old Russia, martyrs were always revered and they are deeply etched in the national memory to this day. Furthermore, a deep abyss was created between the governing body and the people. People who are not experienced in the complexities and strategies of politics and have forgotten what it is like to be respected, like a tuning fork, eagerly respond to anything that is even the least bit consonant with their own hopes and interests.

Our political culture is definitely on the mend. In a matter of months, we noticed and recognized gifted people who had always existed but could not show themselves during the years of ideological despotism. And those are just gifted people! Had a political genius like Lenin emerged during the Khruschev and Brezhnev years of "true Leninism," at best he would have been exiled to Siberia. Incidentally, the czarist autocracy was much more lenient toward its outspoken critics than was the subsequent authoritarian regime to its opponents. Brilliant luminaries of current famous public figures (such as deputies S. Alekseyev and A. Sobchak), are the direct product of Perestroika. And while they have always maintained their creativity, now their work has greater repercussions and the benefits they bring to the country are much more visible than before.

In politics, as in sports, it is easier to win a title than

to hold on to it. As Truman wrote in his memoirs that when he became president he found that he was riding a tiger. In the future, Yeltsin will have to put forth a lot of effort to stay abreast of the public interest. The people—who carried him almost to the very top (Gorbachev still is number one), and are ready to carry him on an Asian palanquin—will reject him as their idol the moment they feel that he does not justify their hopes and that, forgive my low style, he is just not cutting the mustard." At the same time, however, you can't bite off more than you can chew.

Yeltsin made a name for himself through his personal qualities at a time when he was highly criticized; but today, when other abiliues ot a constructive type are necessary, these same qualities may clip his wings. A bulldozer operator destroys, while an architect creates. Both are necessary to society. Both can become heroes of labor. But it is difficult for them to switch occupations. The label, "unconstructive critic," has been attached to Yeltsin, though he denies it.

Let us take his proposal to allow private property in our country. He did not come up with this by reading scientific books. He sensed it from the convulsions of a suffocating economy. In this sense, Yeltsin is a populist since he expresses the sentiments of some of the people. He who still calls for educating the masses should learn that he, himself, is a son of the people, not the father, and that it is not the people but the children that must be educated, and not by using out-moded principles.

Other rhetoric is used against private property, such as "we asked the people if they agreed." The trouble is—they did not ask. Then let's have a referendum on this issue and we will act in accordance with its results. So far, however, we are unable to part with the ideological dogma associated with private property; we are like a selection committee that will not permit an applicant to take an entrance exam because of a hidden fear that he might turn out to be the most qualified.

We support several other, extremely important issues put on the agenda by Boris Yeltsin. Millions of Muscovites who mandated him as people's deputy, as well as people living in other parts of our immense country, responded positively to his pre-election program. One of them even gave up his membership in the Supreme Soviet for his benefit. Having closely studied Yeltsin's programs and subsequent speeches, however, one does not get the impression that there is a clear-cut concept of the social development of the Soviet state.

We now have the unique opportunity not only to criticize but to construct new models of social progress, to create new theories, to suggest hypotheses, in a word, to act creatively. And this work cannot be substituted by mechanically collecting popular slogans.

Furthermore, it has become inexcusable to admire the beautiful but lifeless status quo. What is needed now is a constructive dynamic. The disturbing threat of the country breaking up into national components has appeared on the horizon. This significantly complicates our progress. Where is the Yeltsin manifesto that would give food for deep thought, engender debates, conscious approval or rejection? Unfortunately, we have not seen it. If only he would issue it with the same conviction with which he blasts the errors of Perestroika. Lengthy debates on an issue cannot, unfortunately, take the place of a well written, well thought through concept. It is impossible (as the philosopher Zinoviev noted) to reach galactic heights. Of course, you can demand too much of one person, unless he is a leader—in which case we can and we should. I think it was Kissinger who once said something to the effect that the most important qualities for a statesman are courage and will power. Knowledge can be acquired from consultants, but will power cannot be borrowed.

One thing Boris Yeltsin does not lack is will power. So all that is left is a "trifle"—to formulate a concept. Maybe his mini-tragedy is that he stands before an audience of millions without a knowledgeable staff. At any rate, his consultants have not as yet demonstrated the needed qualifications. The economists are in a position to help him significantly as are the people's deputies but it appears that they are consumed by strong political ambitions, though they lack Yeltsin's political charm. Who can deny that there is competition for leadership among the inter-regional deputies? Most likely that is why they were unable to agree on a chairman. One can predict that soon sharp contradictions will surface in this group. They will start arguing about who is more correct (this, incidentally, is the perpetual plus and the dramatic minus of our intelligentsia).

The fact that Yeltsin lacks an intellectual environment, a brain-trust necessary for any politician, drastically worsens his chances as a promising public figure. But such a deficiency is not written in stone—it can be overcome. But at this point Gretchen's question arises (Goethe's "Faust"), a decisive and delicate question, which is equally hard to answer or not answer. Gretchen asks about religion, but we will ask about something else: is it by chance that comrade Yeltsin has no intellectual team? Why does he lack charisma in the eyes of the eggheads, to use a western phrase? Why doesn't he captivate and enlist the aid of the country's brains? Is it because it is much more difficult to charm them? At this point, nobody is in the position to give a complete answer and, least of all, Boris Yeltsin, himself. We will have to wait.

Now, I will touch upon opinions about leadership style. The first autumn of Yeltsin's presiding over Moscow comes to mind. It will long remain in unofficial chronicles. Fruits and vegetables were abundant. Even berries appeared in the stores. Rows of wooden kiosks mushroomed on the sidewalks and in the squares. The general mood resembled the celebration of an especially good harvest. Now, the last kiosks are being torn down and the supply of vegetables in the capital last fall could only be compared to war time. Since we place the highest demands on Boris Yeltsin, we will not compare him with his successor. No reason to be petty. But it would be just as wrong to remain forever grateful for those cantaloupes and watermelons and fail to analyze the situation deeper. The foundation of that wonderful autumn was quite shaky, since it was created by administrative fiat. Everything was done by force, distraction, and worker layoffs. "Some good decisions were made, but they are being sabotaged," announced the first secretary of the City Council, using the same powerful weapons of personal recriminations. It was economic Robespierrism. It is possible to sustain a city with a good supply of imported agricultural goods for one, maybe two years. But then what? The situation becomes the current dreary picture of shortages. Yeltsin had to accept an unusual gift: he was forced to resign. Through this he was able to retain his aura of fame and mysteriousness. In time, however, evidence mounted of downright mismanagement and inefficiency in running the city more populous than some countries. But, since Yeltsin left of his own accord, he is admired. Sagacity is another of his strong points.

Thus, the decisions so lauded at the time turned out to be unsatisfactory, which is why it took a fist to pass them in the first place. You can terrorize an entire country, declare war on another nation and utterly defeat it, but you cannot bring down your own economy and get away with it. The more coercion in the economy, the less effective it becomes. Some economists who have clung to their ideas of further perfecting socialist planning, and who are now beginning begrudgingly to support a market economy, can be forgiven for their ignorance of this fact. But a candidate for leadership on a grand scale must be fully aware of the possibilities and limitations of power.

There is another type of economist who recently did the government a dubious service by advising it to pass a resolution that would pay farmers for grain in dollars. At the recommendation of scientific experts, the ruble is being attacked. This is not being done with any evil intent, but is simply the result of economic ignorance. The fact that everyone is obsessed with the desire to acquire dollars is pushing the ruble out of the domestic market, which only complicates and further postpones achieving the goal of a convertible monetary unit. The contradictions in official policies are glaring. On the one hand, we are establishing the prerequisites for at least a partial convertibility of the ruble and are talking about a foreign currency auction; and on the other hand we are gathering forces of an opposite polarity. We then bring the two together, which is like stepping on both the accelerator and the brakes at the same time while driving a car.

This slight digression from the main topic was necessary to illustrate the duality of Yeltsin's dilemma. It is easy to get advisors, but it is vital that one gets the right advisors.

Boris Yeltsin repeatedly demonstrated the boldness of his ideas. For the sake of establishing democracy he broke many taboos which we had assimilated with our mother's milk. Nonetheless, to this day, his political credo is unclear. What comes from his mouth is fragmented and disconnected, rather than just left unsaid. It is doubtful that anyone questions his openness. After all, he shared without hesitation the dispiriting news that he began to realize the shortcomings of the administrative-command system only after he was ensconced in the Politburo and saw the different levels of Soviet life. Truly a case of better late than never. Many of our heroes who worked in the regional administrations, ministries, party committees, and departments had for decades continued to believe that they had furthered the cause of socialism, even as they left the stage. Yeltsin's visit to the United States allowed him to make another discovery regarding our self-deception. Of course by now, even school children have stopped talking about it in whispers. No doubt Yeltsin was not the only one among the ruling comrades past and present who made such a discovery. But he was the only one who did not remain silent. His opinions about the political structure of the Soviet Union suffer from contradictions. It must be pointed out once again that what he has is a collection of views on various issues. What he does not have is a complete system of thought. A politician must be predictable and controllable to prevent us all from once again ending up under the wheels of history.

Let us not predict the outcome of Yeltsin's career. As of now, it is in his hands. Giving him respect where it is due, we must not lose sight of the fact that the phenomenon of Yeltsin became possible only as a result of the phenomenon of Gorbachev. (End of article, October, 1989.)

Let the reader judge for himself whether or not we ended up under the wheels of history. This article came to the notice of Yeltsin's group, which at the time consisted of "nomina obscura," unknown people who thought the article was not at all derogatory and possibly even favorable. Nonetheless, the doubts I had expressed about predictability aroused disapproval and suspicion towards me.

Be that as it may, signs of suspicion by Yeltsin's group still remained when, in 1990, I became a member of the presidential consulting council. During the fall of that same year, Yeltsin visited Sakhalin in the capacity of Chairman of the Supreme Soviet of Russia. I had relocated to Sakhalin not long before to become chairman of the regional Executive Committee. The three days we spent together in Sakhalin and plus the flight we shared to the southern Kuril Island of Kunashir, evidently did not leave Yeltsin with the impression of hopelessness (not the worst impression) about the author of these words. Soon after, G. Burbulis called me and asked if I would agree to become a member of the higher consulting-coordinating council of the Presidium of the Supreme Soviet of Russia. I agreed. After Yeltsin became president, he reorganized this body into the Presidential Council. The Council rarely adjourned, and I flew in to attend the meetings less and less frequently, since I considered their proceedings to be unimportant. In addition, it was geographically inconvenient for me. I was relieved to hear from this same Burbulis in April of 1992, that my membership in the Council had been terminated.

So, those surrounding Yeltsin viewed me with a critical eye, especially since later on I did not have the reputation of an ardent supporter, and did not seek it. But, I was not an opponent, either. On a personal level I find him likable. He is frank and devoid of deceitfulness. Since I am from Siberia, I view him as a fellow-countryman and, all things being equal, I would give my preference to him.

He also has certain qualities necessary for a prominent political figure. He is a patriotic politician, which is something that cannot be said about many of his ministers and counselors.

He has a remarkable memory. When he asked for statistical data on Sakhalin prior to his trip there, I did not take it seriously, thinking that he wouldn't really need to know how many hospital beds or tons per hectare there were. Yet, it was precisely these kinds of figures that he quoted without notes and without hesitation. He was able to name the average income to within a half-ruble. The only statistic he did not refer to was the capacity of steam baths, and that was only because that information was not in the packet. I witnessed how this natural gift helped him in many other cases. Furthermore, he is well experienced in life. You can't catch an old bird with chaff, and those ministers that tried to do it once did not dare to do it again after being raked through the coals. I will not go on listing the traits of a statesman that he possesses; I have already mentioned the ones that will be useful later on.

A question of ethics arises at this point: How can a former governor pick apart his former boss? It can be done, and I do not have any qualms about it because I was never indebted to Yeltsin or to anyone else. When I began my fight for Sakhalin in Moscow in

1985, seeking the right to implement the changes that I brought about in the following three years, Yeltsin was the party secretary of the Sverdlovsk region and had professed different opinions. Also, I became chairman of the regional executive committee with the firm intention of changing over to a market economy before he became the Chairman of the Supreme Soviet of Russia; consequently, I was not knocking on the king's door for a job. The fact that, he re-assigned me as head of the regional administration after the Sugust putsch does not change anything either. That only confirmed the status quo. As for my title, with my first decree, dated October 14, 1991, I changed it to Governor and renamed my assistants as Vice Governors. After that, local deputies began a writing campaign demanding that I be fired for arbitrariness. The president himself was also unhappy. In answer to one of my letters which I had signed as Governor, he informed me, "I would also like to bring to your attention the discrepancy between the title you use on your letterhead and your official title. I would ask you to correct this discrepancy" (December 17, 1991). I did not correct it, and still consider "Governor" to be more proper than "Head of the Administration", especially considering the fact that on December 23 of the same year, at a regional meeting, the people's deputies voted for the title "Governor". Eleven months later, when the Union of Heads of Administrations—Governors—was officially registered at the Ministry of Justice, the President congratulated all of his deputies on becoming Governors.

And here is another interesting detail. In contrast to Yeltsin, the President of the USSR, Mikhail Gorbachev, accepted my official innovation immediately. A telegram he sent to me, dated November 19, 1991, was addressed as follows: "To the Governor of the Sakhalin Region, comrade Fedorov, V. P."

Actually, I was a little uneasy about the fact that I went from being an elected official to an appointed one, dependent on the will of one person and his entourage. That is why I supported and continue to support the idea of gubernatorial elections.

Before I begin my analysis of Yeltsin's policies and their current results, it is worth examining the actions of his predecessor.

Gorbachev

Marxist theory foresaw the possibility
that in the course of building a new society it
would be necessary to
start from scratch several times.

M. Gorbachev

Many still remember the time when, in November, 1978, the name M. S. Gorbachev was added to the list of Moscow's highest ranking leaders. Nobody paid much attention to it then; they just noted that this big party appartchik that was transferred from Stavropol, would henceforth be a secretary of the Central Committee, "the agricultural secretary" as they said in the party jargon. Some may even have sympathized with him: to be responsible for agriculture is a risky and thankless job, and in the eyes of the public, of little interest. The situation became similar to that of Polyansky, who was put into the top post of managing our ailing agrarian sector in his day. But he was not able to improve the situation and got no accolades in that position. Like Polyansky, Gorbachev was young (born March 2, 1931) when he ascended the "Party Olympus", but everyone knew that under the existing conditions, his rise did not guarantee him political longevity. The decrepit Areopagus, headed by the "beetle-browed eagle" (from an anecdote about Brezhnev), had to rejuvenate itself, but it did it in a way that posed no threat to itself. It had in Gorbachev an obedient regional secretary (there were practically no disobedient ones in that pre-Yeltsin era). It put him in a secondary position and could at any time demote and transfer him elsewhere on the grounds that he could not handle the job of advancing agriculture. The was a well known fact that nobody could do the job. I think even the ruling geriatrocratic leadership knew it.

Despite his unremarkable initial appearance on the scene in Moscow, Gorbachev's biography catches the attention of the careful reader. It was not because of his two college degrees (in 1955 he graduated from the Law Department of Moscow State University and in 1967 - from the Stavropol Agricultural Institute). At that time it was a common occurrence to find doctors of Science, Corresponding Members and Academicians among the party leadership. Gorbachev's previous career reads as a list of positions, first in the Komsomol and later in Party organizations. It can be used to study the hierarchical structure of the former regional leadership apparatus. From 1956 to 1958, he was the First Secretary of the Stavropol City Komsomol Committee; from 1958 to 1962, he was the Second and then the First Secretary of the regional Komsomol Organization. From 1962 to 1966, he was head of the Stavropol Regional branch of the CPSU; from 1966 to 1968, First Secretary of the Stavropol City Committee of the CPSU. From 1968 to 1970, he was Second Secretary, and from 1970 to 1978, First Secretary of the Stavropol Regional Committee of the CPSU. Then his biography followed the same pattern in Moscow, where between 1978 and 1985 he was a Secretary of the Central Committee of the CPSU; in 1979 he was nominated for membership and in 1980 became a member of the Political Bureau of the CPSU; from 1985 to 1990, he was General Secretary of the USSR; in 1988-1989, Chairman of the Presidium of the Supreme Soviet of the USSR; in 1989-90, Chairman of the Supreme Soviet of the USSR, and in 1990, President of the USSR.

Shortly after his appearance in Moscow you could find buried in the newspapers that Gorbachev had left the sphere of agriculture (this is where I think he demonstrated remarkable political skill) and entered the denser sphere of the Politburo. When Chernenko fell ill, he came close to the very top. I remember two things in particular from that time. One was Gorbachev's speech at an important ideological meeting in December, 1984 (to remind you of the ambiance of that period, the full name of that national scientific and practical conference was The Improvement of Developed Socialism and Ideological Work in the Light of the Decrees of the June (1983) Plenary Session of the CC CPSU), in which he advanced some new and rather bold (for that time) concepts. The press printed only a summary of his speech. I heard it on good authority that Chernenko himself, on the advice of his aides, did not give permission to have the entire speech published (I was acquainted with one of those aides during my graduate years; he dropped a few ranks due to the change of leadership). It is possible that such was not really the case, but the lack of reliable and open information often generates gossip that itself becomes a force working either for or against the top leadership.

For me as well as for others this served as a kind of signal. We started paying closer attention to the actions of the "Second." Also memorable was his trip to Great Britain as head of a delegation of members of the Supreme Soviet of the USSR during the last month of 1984. It was then that Margaret Thatcher made her famous remark about Gorbachev that he was someone you could do business with. She was impressed, among other things, with the fact that Gorbachev agreed with an observation made by the English Prime Minister Palmerston in the last century, that a country does not have everlasting friends or everlasting enemies, it only has everlasting interests. It was unusual to hear this from a communist leader.

This is all preface. The real story begins from the moment Gorbachev became the leader of the party

and the country as a result of the special plenary session of the CC CPSU called in March 1985 following
Chernenko's death. The outcome of that session had
nothing to do with the fact that Chernenko knew
Gorbachev, for he did not know him, or, at best, barely knew him. The real reason behind the choice was
that after the ailing Brezhnev, Andropov and
Chernenko, it was unbearable to imagine another
superannuated figure like Grishyn, Tikhonov or
Gromyko leading the country. I remember seeing a
strange looking man reading the news about
Gorbachev's appointment as General Secretary and
repeating over and over: "He's marked! He's marked!"
This was obviously in reference to the birthmark on
Gorbachev's forehead, but it was clear that the man
had something else in mind: he meant that this leader
would bring us something unexpected. It was a little
chilling to hear such words, but the benevolent-look-
ing, touched-up portrait of the leader had a soothing
effect. After all, what could possibly happen to a country which would unquestionably maintain its stability
for centuries to come, having solved all of its basic internal problems? The only problem it faced was from the
international forces of reaction, with American imperialism in the forefront. But even in that arena, there
were favorable tendencies that should be continued:
the military parity that had been achieved had to be
broken to our advantage (anything was within our

power), and we had to paint more and more new territories on the globe red. Surely, if Carter could not resist Brezhnev and kissed him publicly in Vienna, and by so doing significantly increased the effects of the propaganda banner flown far and wide at the time, in which Lenin himself approved of Brezhnev's policies ("You are on the right path, comrades!"), then Gorbachev would certainly win Reagan over. The new Soviet leader had the advantage over Reagan not only in age but in professionalism as well. That is what it seemed like then.

One of my acquaintances, a Doctor of Political Science, had this opinion on Gorbachev's inauguration: "He's young. He will stay in power for 20-30 years. He'll continue on the old course, changing it in some ways, but not very much. It's boring." But we were destined not to be bored from the very first months of the new leadership. One staggering piece of news followed the other.

Not very long ago, we believed it to be an axiom that a political figure who went through the millstone of the party system became rigid and incapable of revolutionary initiative and change. This axiom turned out to be false. The wheels of a truck do not present a threat to an experienced yoga. A skilled politician does not emerge from the depths of the system to become its prisoner. Imprisonment is the lot of the weak. Other politicians make the system work for them.

Which is no small feat. Few try to do anything extraordinary, such as to reform from the bottom up, or
to destroy the existing system and substitute it with a
new one created with one's own hands. This is precisely the process that Gorbachev started. The entire
administrative system suffered the most severe blows
from the top man and his initially few comrades-in-
arms.

As a Soviet writer stated in 1990 (I believe it was
Pristavkin), it was not the party that created Perestroika,
but one man, alone—Gorbachev. One must agree with
this, as well as the fact that the party offered more resistance than support regarding the cardinal changes.
And when the changes accelerated to the stage of being
revolutionary, millions of fervent communists simply
dropped out as a counter-revolutionary sediment. The
French do not have a monopoly on Vendee.

Future historians will carefully and impartially study
the details of these events that altered the course of
our country's future. They will not have the uncertainty of the moment hanging over them. But we have
our own unique advantage over these future historians. We are the observers and participants of a great
historical process, the beginning of which remains vivid
in our memory. Gorbachev is Russian, and the Russians
have a saying, "Well begun is half done." The Germans
have a catch phrase, "Victory has many parents, but
defeat is always an orphan." In the case of Gorbachev's

success, he immediately gained several self-proclaimed co-authors, aides and prophets. But considering the outcome , he is now forever nailed to the pillory of history. Negative events affect people more strongly than positive ones, and some of today's political journalists portray Gorbachev as a tragic figure. To foresee the future is as desirable a gift as it is unattainable.

The reason I brought up the future was to make the following comment: the lead player of Perestroika - Gorbachev - lacked the gift of prophesy. Being, as we all are, a product of the System, he saw its ugliness, ineffectiveness and, finally, its lack of vitality, and decided to change it. Though he imagined the task to be difficult, he nonetheless believed it would follow a predictable, orderly, and successful course. He followed his own, seemingly indisputable, logic. If you were to substitute the irrational with the rational, the wrong with the right, the results should be quick and positive. The main obstacles on this road would be of a technical nature, (i.e., within the various branches of industry). But the solid power and decades-long Soviet experience were in a position to set the economy on a different track. Especially since the party, the government and the people would focus most of their attention on the economy, no barrier could withstand such a concentrated, massive force.

Alas, that is not how it happened. The economic restructuring was launched under the slogan of acceleration, but instead, a deep economic crisis occurred. It turned the leader's promises and the people's hopes to ashes. It was a miscalculation by his economic advisors, but the responsibility fell on the shoulders of the political leader.

Academician Shatalin admitted in an interview that even after he had become a member of the Presidential Council, he still had not decided for himself whether or not to sell land to the farmers.

What does a market mentality mean? First of all, it is admitting that existing policies have limited maneuverability in the labyrinth of the economy. Under a planned system, agricultural policies always function as a straight jacket (if it is one or two sizes too big, then it is called liberal or democratic), whereas in a market system the actions of the government consist of fine-tuning the agricultural mechanism, which functions on its own. It is easier to change religions, easier to reject God and embrace the devil, than to switch from a planned economy to a market economy, because to do so you must completely change your mentality completely.

We clearly must realize the following: you cannot be smarter, more educated, or more astute than life itself. The function of the government should not be to bind the economy, but rather to overcome (or, even better, prevent) extremes and undesirable digressions. A healthy economic life can be built only in a true multi-sectored structure, one of the inherent elements of which is private property.

"If your own mother won't teach you, life will teach you," as they say in Siberia. If our own Academy will not enlighten our elite with this basic economic commandment, then harsh necessity will. When the stores are empty, the streets and squares are filled. And the people build barricades.

So, after declaring socialist restructuring and confidently predicting that the growth rate would rise from 4.5 to 5% daily, they discovered neither socialism nor growth, but the progressive destruction of the economy. Is this not a parting of between words and actions, or, to continue in the vein of this narration, is this not the absence of insight a quality which leadership should possess?

No less sensational is a retrospective in the area of internal and political democracy. Sometimes looking at the past is no less unsettling than an unknown future. Let us leaf through the newspaper files of the years past in order to test the accuracy of our memory. Launching Perestroika, the initiator wanted to channel it towards economic reform. The need for political reform was either hushed up or mentioned in a faint whisper. He also neglected to express his opinions and publish in a timely manner the results of a full study of the bloody history of our country since 1917. Why bother? It would take up too much of society's time and energy, and is useless, anyway. You can't feed yourself with the past. We need this energy to create the present. Nor did Stalin ever appear in Gorbachev's speeches as a monster that should be tried (not by history, which had already condemned him, but by a regular court). Rather, he was characterized as a builder of socialism who allowed things to go off track. "And so, the main ruling body of the party, headed by J. V. Stalin, vindicated Leninism in the ideological war. It formulated a strategy and tactics during the first stages of the construction of socialism. The political course was approved by the majority of the party members and the workers." (From Gorbachev's speech, November 2, 1987). You cannot make an omelet without breaking eggs. To tell the truth, a careful mention of Bukharin (one of the "eggs") in a positive light cast a shadow on the restrained evaluation of the work of the leader of all time and people.

Clearing away the debris from history's ash heap, including the seemingly impossible restoration of the true image of Trotsky, became inevitable during the natural course of social events and the inseparability of economics and politics. But the leader wanted to do precisely that—to separate one from the other. We were discovering truths long since known to the civilized world. The first step towards our realizing one such truth was mastering a key postulate: the economic effectiveness we are striving for is not compatible with political ossification. Thus we began eliminating the latter. It seemed that all that was necessary to accomplish this was simply to loosen the reins a bit. But that turned out not to be the case. It became clear that political healing must include eliminating the political monopoly.

Another aspect of Perestroika could be mentioned: how we started the fight against mass alcoholism and how we ended it. Social phenomena, such as drinking, laziness and thievery, have deep roots. To reduce them takes time and carefully formulated actions that go just as deep. The smallest success would mean colossal self-improvement in our society. But the CPSU (Communist Party of the Soviet Union) in a doctrinaire fashion, rejected a compromise of realistic minimum proposals and only accepted the maximum. Not cutting down on drinking, but eradicating it completely! Period, end of story! We gained speed and ran our heads against a stone wall. The thoughtless anti-alcohol, rah-rah campaign turned out to be so scandalous that the instigator prefers to keep silent about it to this day. We can only hope that the current leadership will learn its lessons in dealing with social phenomena, which cannot be changed by sending in the cavalry.

To avoid the risk of boring the reader, I will give just one more example from a long list of Perestroika themes. It was impressed upon us that the German question would be resolved by time, a hundred or so years in the future. In the meantime, the two German states would stand firmly side by side, and any attempts to undermine the sovereignty of the GDR (German Democratic Republic) was fraught with serious consequences. Unexpectedly, the independence of the GDR evaporated before our very eyes and the unification of the two Germanys took place. The Soviet Union lost control of the process. "History had started moving with unexpected rapidity." This came from the mouths of the highest leaders who assured us of a century-long status quo.

The essence of one of Yeltsin's polemics addressed to Gorbachev given after he had shaken off the old harness and revolted, was that when restructuring began there was no plan of action nor an analysis of its consequences. Gorbachev defended himself as best he could without naming his critic, to avoid popularizing the latter in his speeches. He refuted the criticism and even named the actions that were planned. Then, Gorbachev's famous long article, "The Socialist Concept and Revolutionary Perestroika," made a fast appearance. The following is an excerpt where he quickly regrouped his arguments.

"There are some who are attempting to accuse us of not having a clear, detailed plan for implementing the concept of Perestroika. I do not think it possible to agree with such a statement. I believe we would be making a theoretical mistake if we were once again to force upon society ready-made schemes and force life itself into the 'Procrustean bed.' This was characteristic of Stalinism, and we do not want to follow in his footsteps. We are acting according to Lenin. And, to act according to Lenin means to research how the future evolves out of current reality. We will make our plans according to that." ("Pravda," 11/29/89) . Lenin did not have a complete program of building socialism in our country and neither do we. This is one of the main conclusions the author makes. We must, he says, remove the fetters from our progress. It will find the right direction on its own; it will create a program of its own accord, post factum, so to speak. You never can see how things will develop ahead of time.

The situation prompted the eternal question: who is right? The philosophical answer in this case is clear. The solution lies somewhere between these two extremes. It is true that there is little that can be foreseen, and Gorbachev became convinced of this from his own bitter experience. To program your course of development, as Yeltsin demanded, to sort everything in an orderly fashion is possible theoretically, but it will not produce the desired effect. System mentality definitely outweighed market mentality in this case. But Gorbachev was vulnerable as well. How could you talk about comprehensive development if the main spring - a free market - was not being wound up? Instead, what we had were prohibitions, deviations, and half-measures. While one person demanded we charge (in reality drain) the economic energy with a detailed program, the other hoped to generate energy by stepping on the brakes. One fastened a chain to the greyhound's collar, while the other was pulling it by the tail. The results, I believe, are about the same, although both desperately wanted the greyhound to run faster.

It became clear later on, however, that Yeltsin did not have a program either when he came to power. The changes that Gorbachev set in action brought about such overwhelming and unexpected results that, had he known of them ahead of time, he might have wavered and lost his resolve and chosen the worst-case scenario - a return to the old ways of his predecessors. Would he wittingly have assumed the responsibility for the collapse of the Soviet Union, world communism, and friendly regimes; for giving in without firing a single shot to the "most evil enemy of them all - capitalism and imperialism," for the pulling down of Lenin's monuments? I am not so sure. Academician Landau once said something to the effect that the method is more important than the results. It goes without saying that the results are as good (or bad) as the method. Gorbachev's method was as bad as they get, and very dated.

Wandering and Windfalls

There are laws of nature.
Adam Smith applied them to society
and someone, for convenience, called this capitalism.

(International Economic Conference
Kriens-Montana, Switzerland,
June, 1991)

U nder no circumstances should statesmen be the-
orists. These types of people pose a threat. In
order to satisfy their theoretical ambitions, they view
society not as an independent value, but as an object
of action. They are worse than certain military com-
manders who, out of principle, are ready to send their
last soldier to his death to, say, put up the flag on a certain hill. Social theories are not reliable. They always
conceal defects. But the ones who end up suffering
are not the creators of these theories, but ordinary people. The example of Lenin, who was both the cre-
ator and implementor of his theories, should serve
as a fundamental lesson for all time. But, neither
should statesmen become intellectually trapped. They
should not feel inferior in the face of various opinions
and authorities. We all lived under the Soviet system.
We believed in it and behaved accordingly. Even then,
however, Yeltsin displayed inexplicable behavior. Take,

for example, his speech at the 27th Congress of the CPSU. "The delegates might ask me, why did I not mention this in my address at the 26th Congress? I can answer and answer honestly: I guess I did not have enough courage and political experience." And when Yeltsin realized that the system tricked him, he acted brilliantly—he attached the system head-on. Only a heroic few can be compared to him in this. But having tossed Marxism-Leninism out of his head, he needed a new philosophical compass. Since he did not have one, he made contradictory statements, was indecisive, and generally did not know where to start. He was surrounded with so many different advisors with all kinds of degree and credentials, that anyone would get lost.

My observations tell me that when he first became Russia's leader, Yeltsin hoped to find the way through consultations with learned economists. But it turned out that the Doctors of Science, the Corresponding Members and the Academicians were all at odds with each other and were in no condition to reach a consensus. And most amazingly, he found, they could change their views, and more than once. Yeltsin did not expect such indecisiveness from the scholars. I remember Gorbachev had the same complaint. He publicly proclaimed his disappointment in the science of economics and one after the other changed his economic advisors—first Aganbegian, then Abalkin, Shatalin, Petrakov, and Yavlinsky, who served as a consultant for a very short period. A joke circulating in the West at the time was that Gorbachev knew full well that among his one hundred economic experts there was one that was giving him sound advice and that he had asked the CIA to find that one expert.

What those in power are currently doing to the economy can only be described by one word—destruction. It is impossible to find a rational explanation for the current policies. Neither the tragic statistical reports, nor the sad facts of economic reality, nor cogent arguments induce Yeltsin to rethink and alter the direction of change that he has taken.

On his way in 1990, Yeltsin liked to repeat a basically correct thesis: "No one—not the politicians, not the academicians—is insured against making mistakes. And if Abalkin makes even a small mistake, it circulates in the economy on a massive scale, and this results in a gross miscalculation." Today, it is no longer L. Abalkin, who was deputy to the Soviet Premier, N. Ryzhkov on questions of reform at the time, but Yeltsin himself who is making the first cardinal error, which is leading to the destruction I have mentioned . I am not repeating this word (destruction) absent-mindedly. Instead of using this word, everyone talks about "reforms", which is a typical euphemism for the real state of affairs.

Eagles don't catch flies. Big people make big mistakes. In order to get to the bottom of this problem,

we must study the psychological phenomenon of
Yeltsin. His transformation from a partycrat to a democrat is a positive phenomenon. Millions and millions
of former party activists and ordinary citizens went
through the same metamorphosis—they traded in their
socialist ideology for a market one. But it is not they—
or, rather, we—that are to blame. It is the regime that
forced its value system on to us from early childhood,
and held us in its grips to old age. In retrospect, the
changing of convictions on such a mass scale proves
that the previous ideology, which produced such a typically Soviet social trait as hypocrisy, was unconvincing
and feeble. As soon a communist totalitarianism collapsed and freed its slaves, they started professing normal views.

Everything in moderation—the wise teach us. A
tragic accident took place with Yeltsin's transformation. He multiplied his previous world outlook by
minus one. Or to use another analogy, he turned it
180 degrees. He would not admit to continuity or to
the evolutionary qualities of the economic events. This
inner change in Yeltsin did not escape the keen eye of
Margaret Thatcher. She noted in her memoirs: "I was
amazed that Yeltsin, in comparison with Gorbachev,
had freed himself from communist thinking and language". During the fascist regime in Germany, those
who were brave told the following anecdote: At an
international medical symposium, doctors from around

the world shared with their colleagues the successes of their national medicine. When it came turn for the German specialist to speak he said: "Our achievements are unique. All Germans had their brains replaced and nobody has noticed it."

Nobody replaced Yeltsin's brain. He did it himself and immediately landed in a hostile environment. Reality did not change polarity. He took this task of changing reality upon himself. Having formulated his motto, "everything immediately and now". He began his search for comrades-in-arms. This was not an easy time. He was wracked by doubts. Everything was new. He had to get used to the role that was bestowed upon him. His alliance with Ivan S. Silaev was not bad, and one can only regret that Silaev left the stage so rapidly. My positive thoughts about him are strangely combined with an inexplicable mimicry of Silaev as soon as he took on a different job. Just yesterday he was fighting to give the RSFSR more rights, but after assuming his position in the newly created chair of the CIS he demanded that those same rights be cut. I recall how everyone was speechless. Be that as it may, Silaev could not completely satisfy Yeltsin due to the lack of radicalism in his approach to the detraction of the inherited system. Prime Minister Silaev seemed a little conservative to the revolutionary boss.

The Young and the Smart

Yeltsin suffers when he cannot understand something. But when he gets it or thinks he does, it is impossible to hold him back from taking decisive actions. Having just rid himself of one extreme, he embraces another just as readily and seeks those who would carry out his will.

This was the backdrop to when Yeltsin stumbled upon Gaidar and his team, who proceeded to speak "words sweeter than Mozart's music" These words of Tomskii from the opera, "Queen of Spades", are very appropriate. To be sure. Everyone was frightened at the prospect of the transition to a market economy, and here someone comes along with a very simple recipe: the government must set everything free, prices above all, and remove itself from the control of the economy, and then a miracle will happen, everything will start working on a new basis of its own accord, and in a very short period of time, to boot. The newly emerged romantic cohort seriously thought that to switch to a market economy was enough just to throw away the reins and everything would just happen on its own.

Can non-specialists create an airplane or a car? This is a rhetorical question, since the answer is obvious: Of course not, and no responsible person would ever attempt it. In order to manufacture complicated technical equipment, one needs theoretical knowledge, accumulated by several generations and tested.

Social phenomena are more complex than technical phenomena. Building a market economy is a task of such complexity that nothing can compare to it. And in our country, the wrong people tackled this task.

During a decisive period in history, power ended up in the hands of newly emerged experimenters who began forging their way through to a market economy. By market economy they understood a simplified state of the economy as described in the first volume of Marx's "Das Kapital", which depicted the conditions in England one hundred and fifty years ago.

Yeltsin chose Gaidar and his group. Once Yeltsin called Egor T. Gaidar a smart person. I must digress a bit at this point. When the last Shah of Iran was on the run abroad and correspondents asked him if he was planning to return to Teheran to face the court, which the new leadership there promised would be fair, the Shah replied: "A lot has been said about me, but no one has yet called me a fool." The same goes for Gaidar. But a smart man does not always do the right thing, by far. It is frequently the other way around. Let us take an extreme example. A clever criminal is much more dangerous than a simple-minded one. The important thing is, what is the social face of the statesman like? The Soviet system was insidious in that it mobilized the best intellectual and creative forces in all spheres; it exploited the creme de la creme of its people to support itself. If it were not for that, it would have fallen a lot sooner.

There is no arguing that Gaidar is not void of competence. We have all read his brilliant articles in "Kommunist" and "Pravda", and the concept of an economic turnover in Russia that he offered was a continuation of academic work, his dissertation. But all of the ideas he expressed earlier must be understood as their opposite after he came to power. He charmed Yeltsin with his optimism coupled with his formulas. "Please be patient for six to eight months. Support the president and the president will support you," Yeltsin addressed the people. There was no shrewdness in these words. He honestly believes in what he says. And he bared his soul when he announced that the government was not hiding its plans to liberate prices beginning on January 2, 1992. The people were told ahead of time, and they had time to stock up on some things before the prices jumped. This is characteristic of his humanness, but basically what we have here are anti-market actions. The manifestation of market tendencies, which the president wants to see implemented immediately, were delayed for as long as the bought-up items would last.

In early 1992, Yeltsin traveled across the country. In Ulyanovsk he said: "Yesterday I was in Saratov. I thought they were going to throw rotten eggs at me, but they greeted me with smiles." Perplexed, he shrugged his shoulders. He was, of course, expecting a certain amount of discontent among the people as he lifted price restraints, but the belief that in six to eight months everything would get better overshadowed the fears. Days, weeks, months went by, and the economy kept falling and falling. The lifting of price controls did not solve a single major problem, but what it did create directly or indirectly were new colossal difficulties.

In the case of the "new and the intelligent" public figures that Yeltsin brought to the fore, a curious situation occurred. While the technocrats, boiling with energy, committed and in some ways continue to commit worthless deeds of economic hooliganism, the democratic contingent focuses on their personal virtues. These virtues might be quite significant, but the question is, do they have anything to do with their work?

You cannot start learning after you take a high-ranking position. You have to come prepared. However, these people, headed by Gaidar, who appeared in 1991, came face to face with a difficult economy. They had to figure it out, but studying it could take years. What did they do? Oh, no, they themselves did not rise to the complexity of the economy, they began dropping it to their level of understanding. They started destroying it. Their logic was, if the chair leg is too long, cut it down a bit. As a result, while Western experts compare managing the economy to a military operation and recommend learning from the experience of military history, we have lost all control of our own economy and of the government enterprises. In the mean time, the demands of managing the economy in a transitional period are much higher, and the whole art of economics is much more complex, than under a planned system or in an established market economy. It is pitiful that in this crucial time in our history, preference is given to the primitive policy of deliberate destruction of the previous productive potential. "Let the old burn in the flames of reform; the new is created by the same flames"—such is the motto of our reformers, to state it as clearly as possible.

We do not need just a market economy or a market frenzy. What we need is a social market economy. The word "social" is not added as a catch word. We are talking about different positions. In the center of a social market economy stands the ordinary person and his family. But in a market economy everything is controlled by the newly rich. Both legal and illegal, along with those bureaucrats connected with them. That makes up ten to fifteen percent of the people that voted for the reforms.

Not long ago people were talking about the neo-liberal West German Chancellor Erhard and his reforms in the 40s and 50s. But let us analyze what we said in his book, "Prosperity for All."

"...We will have to come to grips with the fact that in the middle of the Twentieth century, the possibility of significantly relieving the government of responsibilities is unlikely..." (p. 18). And now it is already the end of the Twentieth century.

What Was Done

Effective January 2, 1992, a price ceiling was established for certain consumer goods, that had doubled or in some cases tripled the previous fixed prices. The prices on all other goods and services were left to the influence of market forces, or to be more precise, to the manufacturers, who increased prices ten- to twenty- fold, or, in some cases, even more.

We should have begun the reforms without liberalizing the price structure because our industry is intensely monopolized and the manufacturers have no incentive to increase production. They can get maximum profit in a less arduous way, i.e. through unimpeded price raising. Soon after, the government realized its miscalculation in predicting price fluctuations. The actual situation excelled all expectations. The current leadership found the following excuse. They said that, naturally, they knew that the prices were going to sky rocket, but they did not want to frighten the public, because then they would have swept everything from the stores. This is the social face of the new leadership. If they new that the prices would increase tenfold and more, they should have openly told that to the public instead of deceiving them. In this instance they meld with the bad traditions of the former Soviet leaders, who ruled through lies and deception. And if their expectations of the "insignificant" price increases were not met, they should have admitted that they made a mistake, instead of wiggling out of the situation.

Another miscalculation is of a more long term nature. The government is waiting for the prices to finally stabilize. It will have to wait until the Cows Come Home. The prices will not drop and they will not stand still, they will continue to increase.

No matter how grave they were, the above mentioned defects in the policies were the result of the main strategic mistake: the decision to liberalize the prices. Justifying its course of actions, the government gave the following argument. The most logical thing was to privatize property first and then liberalize prices. But privatization is a long difficult process and the people are already tired, so the liberalization of prices will accelerate the process of switching to a market economy. The road to hell is paved with good intentions. By changing the order of events the government jeopardized the entire economy, which lost its administrative manageability but did not gain a market one.

But that is not all. The essence of switching to a market economy is not only in privatization or de-governmentalizing, i.e. in the changing of the form of ownership. The main thing is to de-monopolize industry and its branches and this cannot be achieved simply by privatizing. Privatization signifies transferring state ownership to private hands. But with a deficit in production and in the sphere of consumer services, the market monopoly can not be dissolved even by privatization, and there will be no competition among them. That means that the amount of private owners and new manufacturers must be increased. Then they will start competing and this will lead to favorable results. Consequently, the government should have thought of long term effects in any case even if privatization were to happen rapidly, as if somebody waved a magic wand. The all encompassing deficit inherited from the administrative command system can be slightly reduced, but not eliminated, by changing the form of ownership. New manufacturing plants must be created concurrently. The whole industrial structure needs to grow parallel to the changes. Three 'F's" characterize this growth: new forms, firms, and farms. They form a hitherto unknown competitive atmosphere in the economic life and make it rational. The parallel structure includes the organization of new reproductive links between the manufacturer and the consumer. The new enterprises or, to use the old terminology, the private structures must grow absolutely and relatively, and they must continuously include new spheres, from which the government will withdraw. My fundamental position is that with time, the government must direct its energy as an owner at the development of a broad infrastructure. This includes some modes of transportation (railroad, city), communication, engineering, science and the military-industrial complex. Only the government can take responsibility for this infrastructure that demands huge up-front investments with no guarantee of future profitability. Maintaining this central structure of state industry at the right level by means of the government will allow us to guarantee economic safety of the country and to have a stabilizing effect on the economic conjuncture, leaving to the private sector the production of various goods and services, agriculture, trade, etc. But the creation of new manufacturing plants takes time. It is a tedious task, even old-fashioned to many, which is why the new leadership let it slide, and thus worsened the economic situation. There is no arguing that we could not maintain the old industrial system, which is why we needed to create the conditions for its rebirth into a more effective economy. The best constructive way to change the old system is by annually decreasing by 10 % state contracts starting with 70%. Possibly in a few years we could have lowered that rate to 5%, since every new step would take a lot of effort. Manufacturers and state industry as a whole would be able to handle their new freedom of 10-15% and would be able to prepare themselves for the next year. We needed to carefully dismantle the existing industrial system by selectively privatizing certain manufacturing plants (adhering to the rule "hands off of efficient plants").

This agenda would allow the old system to maintain a steady level of the basic production of goods. There would be no demands for increased production. The new plants would create an overall increase in production. Neither of these two tasks were fulfilled. What is even worse, the new private entrepreneurs have to be protected from their own government.

On December 23, 1991, I sent President Yeltsin the following telegram: "Dear Mr. Yeltsin! In this, my last attempt to convince you to prevent Russia from falling prey to economic chaos, I urge you to forgo liberalizing prices on January 2, 1992. This measure will cause impoverishment of the people on a mass scale. The increased deficit will force us to ration resources and goods. This will affect the transfer to a market economy. I believe the only right way out of this crisis is to implement a 70% state production manufacturing contract, with further annual reductions of 10%." (Earlier, on October 30, 1991, I spoke at the Fifth Congress of the Peoples Deputies of Russia and I was one of the few who criticized Yeltsin's proposed program of price liberalization).

Of course the telegram did not change anything and in 10 days the price ceiling was lifted.

Where did the figure 70% come from? Yeltsin, himself, named it! I presented my proposal to him during a meeting in his office in 1991, and I offered to start with 90%. "Not 90%, but 70%" he immediately responded, and began writing. "No need to write anything, I put it all down in this note." I then handed him the text of the proposal. I did not argue about the 70%, since I thought it was an acceptable rate. A lot later in 1992, when I heard him say at a meeting of the Presidential Council that every percent contracted to the state is a return to the Soviet Union, I realized that it is useless.

Neither the liberalization of prices nor the privatization of property will ensure a balance between supply and demand in the near future. This balance can be achieved by a rational combination of remaining government manufacturing plants and private companies and by creating new powerful structures on a private basis. So far, the only thing the government has done is redistribute the property, and that is obviously not enough.

By eliminating all barriers from the path of prices, the government is facing the inevitable lowering of living standards for a significant part of the population. It is taking some preventative measures. But they are clearly insufficient for the consumers to maintain their status quo, and that is not their goal anyway. The goal of the highly advertised social protection is the prevention of basic hunger in the country.

Justifying the liberalization of prices by pointing out that goods finally did appear on store shelves does not hold up to criticism. What increase in products can they be talking about when the overall production level has dropped? Where are the products coming from, and in mass quantities? But you cannot argue with the fact that products are filling the stores and anyone can buy them. But not everyone can. Lately the stores have become merely an exhibition of goods for many people. They do not sell because of their prohibitive prices. It used to be that part of the goods were sold through the back door while the stores were filled with lines. Now the stores are full of space and the rich can always find anything they need. The price liberalization made many consumer goods inaccessible to the ordinary people. Consequently the demand lessened and this affected production, the most sacred part of the economy. This concerns predominantly the production of consumer goods and not the arms industry. Nonetheless, during the first stage of reforms the main concern should have been the production of groceries or, according to ancient Greek mythology, the first stages of reform should have been implemented under the sign of Hestia who's responsibilities included procuring provisions.

To free prices in a monopolized economy that is burdened with the military-industrial complex as well as the raw-material industries is completely reckless and possibly ill-intentioned behavior. And this recklessness that started January 2, 1992, feeds on itself, to boot. The decline in domestic productivity is leading to the reduction of goods offered, but this deficit remains invisible, since the ever-rising prices make many every day consumer goods luxury items for a large portion of the population. The import of consumer goods is celebrating its heyday and delivering the final blows to domestic production. Since it is only the people who are poor, the government asks Western countries for credit and they offer it under the condition that Russia will continue with its absurd economic policy. And then it starts all over again.

Some manufacturing plants and even some branches of the Produce Industry are inoperable. The natural resources of the country are being depleted. To mend the damage and move forward will take huge financial resources, which will have to be found. We cannot tolerate this humiliating situation in which millions of people are forced to fight for their physical survival simply because they literally cannot afford groceries.

One characteristic of a developed market is a definite segmentation, in other words, the market is aimed at satisfying the demands of customers of all income levels. Rich and poor alike can purchase products in accordance to their means. Each category of product has tens and hundreds of brands that differ in price, quality and other aspects. Our planned economy was not able to resolve the problem of production and consumer differentiation in its time. There was a saying, "washing out the cheap variety." Things are not much better in that aspect of the economy in this transitional period either. People with low incomes frequently cannot purchase vitally important products at an affordable price.

The tremendous price increase brings manufacturers to the brink of bankruptcy. The mechanism is simple. The increased cost of raw materials and everything that is included in the cost of production, plus the astronomical taxes on the final price, which makes the products inaccessible to the people, leads manufacturers to become over-stocked. Consequently, they lower the production rate and lay off personnel.

When the production rate goes down as a result of economic policies, there is no need to prove that the policies are wrong. The current situation is already characterized by a series of failed companies, but the real crises will manifest itself a little later, when the number of closed down plants will run into the hundreds.

The government is addressing the consequences (by means of their barely perceivable, inadequate support of the consumers), but not the main reason of the disaster (the decreased production). It is as if instead of giving a patient with tuberculosis medicine, a doctor gives him rouge.

Actually, bankruptcy among manufacturers is a usual occurrence in a market economy, but the bankruptcies occur as a result of competition in a saturated market. The companies who fall behind cannot make it. This increases the industry's effectiveness. Bankruptcy in our situation is caused only minimally by the demands of the market. Alas, they fall victim because their own government is shooting them down.

A number of comparisons were made to the method in which we liberalized prices. For example, it was said that you cannot pull a tooth out over a period of weeks. But, by uncapping price growth, we did not remove the bad tooth at all. Instead we just applied pressure to it, thus increasing the pain. No nation, not even such a tolerant one as ours, can withstand this pain endlessly.

Currently, the pressure on the government has increased in connection to its economic course. But we should not criticize only the executive body. The concept of a rapid transition to a market economy, related to the liberalization of prices was once approved by the Fifth Congress of the Peoples Deputies of the RSFSR and by the Supreme Soviet. Some current critics should be reminded of their position prior to January 2, 1992, and of the fact that they are the ones who promoted the hazardous course of leaping into the sea of market economy. And now they are disassociating themselves from the government, fearing responsibility and counting on the short memory of the public.

The Polish version of falling into the market was

unacceptable to us, though it is quite possible that in a matter of years Poland will improve its well-being through shock therapy. We need to evaluate the Polish experience correctly. We must not forget the previous events, that in 1981 Poland switched from a planned economy not to a market, but to a martial law. The subsequent years were lost. The people experienced all the worthless methods of overcoming the crisis and Poland had nothing left but to try the last resort: throw itself into the whirlpool of the market.

We have already forgotten that even before Gaidar, the government was preparing public opinion to an instantaneous change to market relations. In I.S. Silaev's government program to stabilize the economy and switch to market relations the main thesis was as follows: "There is only one possible conclusion: a gradual change from a planned economy to a market one is impossible," But in effect the government's policies were restraining. When Gaidar's cabinet took over they rushed headlong toward the free market.

What does changing an economic system imply? First of all, it is the inevitable disintegration of the existing industrial mechanism on the territorial and branch levels with its subsequent integration into a new form. The art of politics is to do this in an optimal way without destroying the material foundation of the society.

A rational mind cannot comprehend the "clean

slate" policy that was forced on the country, which maintained that the right way is to first tear down the existing economy, with all its components until they are rubble. And the only thing wrong with some of those components was that they existed in the USSR. In an economy that is being totally destroyed not only are thousands of factories and tens of branches of industries become superfluous, but entire regions such as Siberia, Eastern Siberia and the Far East as well. If the first part of the destructive policy takes place under the motto "anything that was not done by us should be cursed," in other words what we have here is the method which has been used repeatedly in history and used by frenzied doctrinaires and dictators—the method of denying the merits of the previous governing body and reviling it. The second part, the building up of the clean slate, this empty field should be called an act of economic snobbism. Who is supposed to do the building, and by what means? Since there are no other resources due to the deliberate destruction, they intend to erect the new economy using the means gained by selling our national natural resources and our national wealth in general, and a leading place among the constructors of our new economy is given to foreign entrepreneurs.

The fact that the government removed itself from economic issues had a grave effect on the military-industrial complex (MIC). Of course the militarization of the industry had reached extreme proportions towards the end of the Soviet period and the issue of cutting back on the MIC was on the table. But the conversion was not well thought out. Instead, production collapsed, which led to serious social problems.

There is another important moment. In the world exports of arms, the USSR held a leading position, competing with the USA. The international community criticized Russia's exporting of arms for political and moral reasons. If Russia had decreased the sales of arms abroad, even if it were forced, that could have initiated an agreement to cut down on arms exports with other leading arms exporting countries. Instead, the competitors filled the gap and nobody is accusing anybody, everybody is satisfied that Russia dropped out as an exporter of arms to the world market. Our Ministry of Defense did not initiate any actions towards tapering arms exports of other countries.

During the past years government policies were aimed at destroying as much of the economy as quickly as possible, including aspects of production or manufacturers or the ties between them. And this work with a minus sign has its ideological basis, which is: to achieve a guaranteed irreversible reform. This policy is too straightforward to be right. The bitter paradox, however, is that by not leaving a single shred of the old system, the government is playing with fire. It is condemning the people to immeasurable deprivation. It is forcing them to nostalgically recall the period of stagnation and to start thinking about returning to the past. The people do not understand what is going on. The material and other deprivations that the people are experiencing are just as unexpected as they are inexplicable to those who lived for many decades under the conditions of more or less satisfied and guaranteed prosperity. The continuation of the course set by the reforms is a risky business.

As the Bolsheviks, (i.e. the extremist confident in their beliefs) distorted the idea of socialism in 1917 and tried to realize it prematurely and in an ugly form, thus discrediting it, so today the radical marketers in Russia bring forth distrust of ideas of market economy in the people with their rash actions. In the eyes of the people, market economy is equated with unbridled price increases, increased poverty, and the government's lack of any social responsibility.

Customarily, Russian economic policies are called monetary policies. It would be more accurate to call them anarcho-monetary. After the communist doctrine with its stern centralism, another experiment is being conducted with the country in the form of practical anarchy. There was a time when anarchic tendencies were wide spread in Russia, however this ideological inheritance was overcome and will doubtfully be in demand again. It proved to be powerless in the face of the complicated development of the means of production on the national and international scene. In our time, what prevails is not theoretical anarchism, which, I repeat, was utterly repudiated, but a primitive primordial force. There is no connection between the studies of Bakunin, Kropotkin and other specialists on this subject, with what is happening with the Russian economy, and there is no sense looking for it. Among other things that would undeservedly intellectually ennoble the actions of the leadership.

The current leadership is mistaken in thinking that their primitive course of actions are leading to the introduction of a market economy, which, they think does not need the governments participation to be created, and, once created, it does not need government control. Sooner or later, this approach (the government's self-removal from playing an active role in the economy) will be rejected and substituted with the constructive actions of those in power to create a market. So now we are not even experiencing a period of transition to a market economy, we are only at the preliminary stages in which the destruction of the production potential of the country dominates.

The government is party to this destruction, not only by what it does not do (more on that later), but also by what it does do. It sees its main task as implementing monetary policies. We immediately went from one extreme to another. Under a planned economy the goal, even the cult, was the growth of production in its pure form. But now production is altogether forgotten. The central focus is on separate monetary figures, separated from production. The analogy with the famous study of Chicago's professor Friedman on monetarism does not hold up, since it is related to a completely different economy and other conditions. Our monetarism comes down to the so called financial stability, which includes, if possible, a low budget deficit and a low inflation rate. They think the rest, will iron itself out. A completely flawed approach. To balance the budget, the government acts as a usurer and lives one day at a time. It collects as many taxes as possible, sometimes the total tax rate exceeds 100%, consequently the entire profit plus all the funds of the manufacturer go into the budget. This eats through the production forces. The producers are being slapped on the hand. I will ask a rhetorical question: does Russia need gold? Obviously it does. Nonetheless, in 1994, for the first time in a long time gold production dropped. But especially interesting are the reasons for this occurrence. First of all, the gold-miners are suffocating from the taxes, secondly, it is obvious that the gold industry is not being sufficiently financed. If the government is not equipped to understand the significance of this precious metal which guarantees the inflationless emission of money, then how can it offer ways to stimulate the production of machinery or children's stockings.

We also vote for balancing finances, but not in the way the government is doing it. It must include not only the macro level but also the micro levels, starting with the finances of manufacturers. You cannot build a healthy government budget by bringing industry to ruin.

The government is acting just as clumsily regarding inflation. There is now arguing with the fact that we must fight it. But this fight must be seen in the context of the general economic situation. Having extracted only one aspect of the economy and labeling it as the number one enemy, the government defies common sense to such an extent that unintentionally doubt in the adequacy of the highest of leaders is increased. For instance, lack of income is destroying production, but the government bureaucrats do not permit the mutual cancellation of debts, for, in their opinion, this will increase inflation. The government does not pay for the orders they place, for the products given to it, partially for the same reason, partially due to a real lack of monetary funds. But with such policies there never will be any money.

Under market conditions there is a concept of a magic polygon, (i.e. solving one problem in the economy makes others worse.) It is impossible to resolve these problems all at once (as one), because their goals (and their are 4-5 of them) are contradictory in nature (i.e. the attempts to solve one problem will aggrandize another one.) For instance, the attempt to stop inflation under certain circumstances can kill production. This has been known for a long time in the West. Under such circumstances the government has to properly choose the most substantial problem at that moment and the right dosage of actions to take in solving it. Our leadership is probably doing both things. The worst thing so far is the dropping of production. While it is disintegrating nothing can be done with unemployment or inflation. The White House on the Krasnopresnenskaya embankment mistakenly considers their priority to be fighting inflation and they are killing production as a result. And time is not teaching it. So you struggled unsuccessfully for four years so stop. Focus on a different task and increase production. But they do not understand that, illustrating a lack of edification, if not worse. Ours is a black polygon. All the figures have a minus in front of them.

So what do we get? In our educated country during a crucial period of time the people who came to power are intellectually limited and socially amoral and they are passing their deranged assertions for universal values. In order to hold on to their power a little longer they spread new lies. I will give two examples. The leadership insists that the standard of living has gone up. And this against the backdrop of poverty and destitution. They try to prove that during 1993 the real monetary income of the population increased by 10%

and that in 1994 this joyous trend continued. Where do they get these figures? They add the profits of entre-preneurs, those 15% who profited from the reforms, to the income of the working class. But 1995 let them down. No matter how they manipulated the statistics, the real profit of the population decreased.

There are different ways of combating poverty. There is the usual way, when rational socio-economic policies are implemented, aimed at increasing pro-duction and the relatively fair distribution of the fruits of the economic growth. But there are others. In his time, a governor of a far-away country annihilated poverty in his city in his own way. At night the police would round up the poor and drown them in the ocean.

Our bureaucrats are not as brutal, but they are not original either. They manipulate statistical data.

Another propagandistic trick consists of promising the people month after month a speedy general eco-nomic stabilization. And, as proof, they once again offer altered statistics. In reality, there is no stability and there can not be any. General economic stabili-ty must be understood as the creation of a new eco-nomic foundation; first a small one, but it must con-tinuously broaden. But this new foundation has not been created. What we will get is not stabilization on a new foundation, but stagnation on the ruins of the old system and on the sickly sprouts of the new one.

What we need is not the freezing of the old economy and not the stretching of the decline to the next century, but positive quantitative and qualitative changes to the domestic production abilities in the near future.

But in the meantime, as a result of faulty policies, Russia has been thrown back many years in comparison with some of its own earlier figures and is losing its position in the international arena. It dropped down to 10th place as far as the gross national product is concerned. In 1970, Russia was in third place, in 1980 in fourth, and in 1990 in sixth place. In other words, not only did the former negative tendency not brake, as we expected and as we were promised, but it increased significantly.

The danger of anarcho-monetary policies is doubling since it is being used during a period of crisis. In the period from 1930 to 1932, during a dramatic decrease in production, the German chancellor Bruning also implemented a policy of leveling the budget and by doing so intensified the problem. After two years of ruling with extraordinary powers he was forced to give his place up to von Papen with his emergency decrees and in a year and a half he, in turn, was replaced by General Schleicher and soon after that Hitler came to power in a completely legal manner.

By leaving industry to fate, our government expects it to be quickly reborn and they are filling us with illusions to that effect. But we have a ways to go until such a time when the market will become a builder of industry. It is entirely possible that by then we will experience not a rebirth of leadership, but the rebirth of a regime. What kind will it be? We do not know yet.

From a temporal point of view, the country has already been led into the phase of active destruction, or finishing off the old system. But it is killing something that is alive, as the old structure has far from exhausted itself completely. Many of its elements are non-transient. Sooner or later we will come to realize this and will partially recreate what has been destroyed and glue together the pieces, cursing our nearsightedness and our new ideological disaster. Just as we used to illustrate everything with references from Marx and Lenin, so do we now justify everything with the same fervor by referring to the market and western scholars. We will also realize that business will not strengthen Russia but will weaken it if we do not give Russian entrepreneurs absolute priority in their own economy.

The country is getting deeper in international debt on the initiative of the government and partially due to the unstoppable force of the wound up mechanism. A new way of paying off the accrued credit is brewing in the super shrewd heads of our politicians. They are planning to hand over our national treasures, or simply stated, our plants and factories, our land and other natural resources, into the hands of foreign states and

```
        UNIVERSITY
        BOOK STORE
   RETAIN THIS RECEIPT
        1997-1998

1  20  98857  824137  Sale

59      Text Sale Books          4.98
                 Subtotal         4.98
            90.0% Discount       -4.48
    Discount code Spec Sale
                Total Tax         0.04
                                 _____

                    Total         0.54 *
                     Cash         0.55
          *** Change Due         -0.01**
18:12 06/22/98

        THANK YOU FOR SHOPPING
     AT UNIVERSITY BOOK STORE
```

businessmen as a loan payment.

This idea needs to be nipped in the bud, because it permits the impermissible. To be precise, the policy for payment allows government's depraved monetary policies with national material wealth that does not belong to it.

The current democrats through their destructive policies have given the word "democrat" a negative connotation among the people. It has become a repugnant term. Democracy cannot be fully fledged if it signifies dictatorship of poverty to the people; if it repudiates national and state interests. Many politicians who came to power after the collapse of communism did not withstand the trial by the fire of power. Their intellectual baggage ended up being insufficient for the requirements. After all the sum of knowledge is a variable figure. The most unpleasant thing, even tragedy, that has fallen on us is that these politicians were mistaken about the object of their actions. They were confronted with an economy completely unlike the economy that they read about in Western textbooks; Economies that have existed not for decades, but for hundreds of years. They were confronted with an economy that was completely governmentalized and monopolized; one that did not accept market mechanism of management to such a degree, that even as it is being destroyed, it still maintains its resistance to market forces.

President Yeltsin said the following words about his cabinet in April of 1992: "The past months have taught the government a lot. It gained unique practical experience, unique knowledge about what the current Russian economy is all about." It sounds like a commendation. In reality it is a denunciation or self-denunciation. It would be logical to ask: "What kind of government starts implementing reforms not knowing what the current Russian economy is all about?" They should not have even started up with the reforms without having professional knowledge. Our country is not a laboratory for testing new inventions and ministry positions are not classrooms for assimilating new subject matter.

Yeltsin's governing differs from Gorbachev's governing in that the General Secretary of the CC CPSU and later the President unwillingly followed the events and was controlled by them, whereas the President of Russia implements change from above and since he does not have a right philosophy, he does not align his actions with the demands of the moment, not in content, nor in priority. Consequently he can not count on success.

They say that during the years of antagonism between the USSR and the USA the Americans developed a plan to rebuild their country after a hypothetical Soviet nuclear attack. Since we did not want to fall behind in anything, an analogous plan must exist in the old Moscow vaults. It is time to unearth it not because of some sort of machinations on the part of the USA, but because the economic safety has been usurped from the inside; we did it with our own hands.

Concerning the democratic contingent that supports the young reformers, they frequently place their ideals above national or state interests, as if we are living in a world of universal brotherhood and as if their invocations of democracy can heat an apartment and feed children. Democrats from the times of ancient Greece did not shun from demagoguery. The infamous Father Gleb Yakunin visited the Southern Kuril island Shikotan. He consecrated this Russian land adorned in a cassock in honor of the significance of the occasion. When he returned to Moscow, he announced that this and the other three islands should be handed over to Japan in order that justice be served. How can one have anything to do with such democrats?

The Positive Aspects

Are there any positive aspects of the past few years at all? There are, but there could have been a lot more given more rational policies.

The private sector that was created from scratch is functioning. This is a completely new phenomenon in our lives. Just recently no one was allowed to have more than six hundredths of a hectare of land for private use. In Siberia and in the Far East a subsidiary hot house for growing vegetables could be no bigger than 15 square meters; if you had 16 the authorities would trample it down with a tractor. You were allowed to have one cow or two, if you had three or four you would be expelled from the party.

With all its shortcomings, privatization laid a material foundation for the creation of a new type of economy. At the same time, scattering the former state property among the people did not lead to higher effectiviency of work at the privatized structures. We skipped the natural stages of development and immediately started at the point were it took Western countries decades and centuries to get to. Nonetheless, state ownership is no longer a monopoly, and over time the secondary privatization by means of buying and selling securities, will lead to the creation of a group of effective proprietors.

The most important result of the reforms in Russia

is that they secured the irreversibility of cardinal changes. The necessary prerequisite for a market system has been met; the beginnings of a free enterprise have been established in the national economy. They are literally beginnings, but it is a dynamic process which is spreading and will eventually predominate in the economy. What does irreversibility of the process mean? It means that the changes cannot be reversed; that if now somebody attempts to turn back it will lead to a civil war. The new proprietors will not give up their positions without a fight and the fight will be on a scale, which will be destructive to society.

Of course the history of our own country tells us that entire classes can be eliminated, to say nothing of a budding beginning. Having compared the vivid results of our planned economy to the market system in other countries we glean our assuredness from practical sense, from rationality. We are confronted with a choice. Either we continue to struggle with the government bureaucracy to continue with the changes, or we face a civil war with all its grave consequences. I hope that we will prefer the first and will continue to move forward.

Another positive aspect of the current situation is that people are now interested in making money. Consequently, they are seeking ways to increase their personal or family budget. This incentive is a result of the fact that a lot of products are now lining the shelves of the stores, due to their significant price increase. In addition, for those families who found themselves below the poverty line, it is a fight for survival. They have no other choice, but to look for additional sources of survival. However, up until now, the reorganization of our economy created the best chance of making money, not through production, but in other ways which most often avoid production.

The new types of proprietary business created are joint ventures, banks, and exchanges. They are the ones who skimmed the cream during the reforms. Now these sources of quick money-making have practically exhausted themselves. New businessmen realize that the only way to ensure financial security is through production. I must make one stipulation here. The free trade law which allowed anybody to sell goods without any limitations, had a two-sided affect on the psychology of the people. On the one hand it acquainted them with market morals, made them develop an interest, even a passion, for money. After several decades of forced monetary Puritanism, and of sanctimoniously belittling private interests, this is a big step forward towards a market education for the society. On the other hand, for a while this will channel the people's energy towards trade, rather than production because it is easier sometimes miraculously easy, to strike gold through unorganized, vulgar trade; whereas production demands hard, systematic work.

Extreme Democracy is a Disaster

Judging by the government and its various ministers and becoming acquainted with their points of view, one would think that they are implementing their own private reforms. But that would not be an accurate evaluation of the current situation. Possibly they succumb to the same mistake. Yeltsin chose them because they are instrumental in carrying on the same destructive work that the President believes to be absolutely necessary. Some cabinet members undoubtedly share their boss's convictions and support them with their own amendments. They bow to the West and cite western scholarly works on economics. The rest are staying in the middle of the stream to protect their careers. If the leadership should change, they will be ready to switch flags and cut back on their rock throwing. Some of the political figures, who are executing the will of the master do not have a single idea or any executive skills. What they do have is an amazing shamelessness as they strive to remain for as long as possible where circumstances have brought them—on the crest of the wave. Once I was shocked to discover that one of the many Vice Premiers in charge of the economy knew nothing about economics, planned or market. It is no joke to learn that a pilot flying the plane you are on was actually trained as a plumber.

The boss tolerates both kinds as long as they continue his line. As soon as they no longer support him, or get tired, they fall into the reject pile, sometimes without a warning. There were instances when high ranking people would learn that they had been fired by reading about it in the paper, or by some other peculiar method, such as the chauffeured car not being there to take him to work one sad day.

Yeltsin's cries for democracy during the demise of the Soviet era made him a national hero and a Kremlin ruler. I will remind the reader that in 1991 the Soviet President Gorbachev gave him a small office in the Kremlin, but soon the saying about two bears in one lair was verified. Yeltsin's democracy, having assumed extreme forms, became an economic disaster for Russia.

The starting point in our transition to the market was absolute state monopoly, which engulfed all aspects of production, turnaround, and management. All these aspects were somehow in concert with each other and year-after-year the mechanism worked worse and worse. When Yeltsin was pondering about "what should be done?" He based his cause on the effect. If the government is the source of disaster for the economy, then it should be removed from it. An attempt was made to do this in the most natural way: the government managing bodies ceased to fulfill their command functions. The result was just as natural—a bad order was substituted with disorder. Enterprises were left to fend for themselves. The government is waiting with hope that their survival instincts of enterprises will wake up market reflexes in them and that the market will appear on its own. Fat chance. The phenomenon of technical-production monopoly is still breathing and making itself known.

From the start, enterprises were planned and created as links in a technological chain. They were created as industrial monopolies. Having gained independence, they have no competitors, since there are either no analogous enterprises or there is a deficit of similar products. So there is no way for them to gain market reflexes, especially since the state, having ill-feelings about government involvement in the economy, lifted all limitations from prices. Enterprises covered their expenses by randomly raising prices. It is a lot easier to raise prices than increase production in order to stay afloat. The infamous cost mechanism, which was criticized back in the Soviet era, has been carried to absurdity during the transition to a market economy. The democrats, who legalized it, are now somewhat surprised that the enterprises still exist, but they still cherish the hope that massive bankruptcies will begin any minute. "Why have they not started yet?" - they ponder. They do not have a clue that it is the entire country with all its people that has gone bankrupt. People cannot keep up with price increases and they live worse than before, they die prematurely . They are the ones carrying the burden of freedom of prices, which turned into a giant sham.

Forced privatization is incapable of abolishing enterprise monopolies. It can only lead to changing types of ownership. Many years must pass before new enterprises will appear and become strong and competitive relations are established in our economy. But almost nothing is being done to create new enterprises. Before they can become strong they need to be created. After January 2, 1992, (i.e. after the liberalization of prices) the conditions for the creation and survival of new market entities have become extremely difficult.

We Need a Demi-Kosygin

The German philosopher Schopenhauer said a strange thing. He claimed that unborn children choose their future parents. Similarly, the future of Russia depends on as yet nonexistent market enterprises, no less than it depends on existing giants such as "ZIL", "Rossel' marsh," and others. The latter were created by the Soviet government as monopolistic entities and as their efficiency, according to international standards, fell as they became larger. Our industrial colossi made the "Guinness Book of World Records" because of their unique size. Now, with the changes that are occurring, these enterprises are doomed to languish for many years to come because of their inability to compete internationally. It is evident what would happen to them if they were to attempt to compete in the world market if we use the example of similar enterprises in the GDR. The East German industrial potential was very respectable according to former socialist standards, but in just two years a major part of it collapsed due to its inability to compete on the world market.

Creating new enterprises is no easy task. It is more of an art. It is easier to do something more concrete, such as rebuilding that which we ourselves destroyed. It feels like we are actually doing something. We are always amazed by the actions of past generations and

by their outstanding historical figures when we can dis-
cern a concern for Russia in their actions. The lack
of perspective in our own thinking and our narrow-
mindedness, not only do not allow us to think of the
future, but actually lead us to destroy today's principles. The period of stagnation and its leaders, such as
Brezhnev, is behind us. But having an impetuous pro-
market, democratic leader is also no blessing.

The market does not just unite, it also separates. It
sets people against one another, makes them competitors and, consequently, divides them into winners
and the losers. Theoretically, if we were to give free
reign to the laissez-faire principle, the basis for a more
or less normal existence would be threatened. A large
part of it would be threatened by degeneration, which
even the famous Scottish free-market economist Adam
Smith (1723-1790) warned against. While we are building our market economy we do not need a Kosygin
or a Reagan, but someone who is half Kosygin and half
Reagan. Moving towards a market economy, the era
demands from the leader of the country or the economy, a rare symbiosis of personal qualities, the main
two being a caring attitude towards the existing productive powers, despite their conservative nature, and
a striving towards a market economy, with a full understanding of all its many defects. Yeltsin only worships
the market and thus cherishes those who echo him.

Demonstrative from this point of view is the five-month duel between the Minister of Finances B. Fedorov and the Minister of Economy O. Lobov, which ended with the latter moving to the Security Council (soon after B. Fedorov also parted with his cushy position). Lobov was a strong Minister of Economy and he will be useful to Russia in any capacity.

In Korea it is customary to respect anyone who has the same last name as yours. They are almost considered relatives. We Russians also take note of those who have the same names. In the beginning, I too treated the young Minister of Finances with sympathy, but later I became convinced that he is merely a narrow-minded manager of financial documents. The completely deficient approach to the economy based on a bare monetary scheme satisfies Yeltsin, so Fedorov practiced it. The less money we have in the economy, the better. This was the guiding principle of the former Minister of Finances and he did everything to realize it. The mutual debts of enterprises forces them to lower production, but the government does not cancel the debts because it thought that this would increase inflation. However, what the government is ignoring is that lowering the production of goods leads to an increase in prices. Inflation continues anyway and in its most malignant form. In the meantime, inflation is sensitive only to one factor, an increased amount of goods on the market. The Ministry of Finances is acting counterproductively by cutting state support for businesses.

Further, raising the lending rate always signifies hard times for business. Western countries revert to this method during a very bullish market, even then the rates are very mild: the discount rate is raised by 1%, 0.5%, or even by 0.25%. Obviously, Russia is not experiencing a bull market, but the rates go up in leaps and bounds and serve as a sure way to suffocate production. The rate itself has become the source of inflation, but the Ministry of Finances keeps talking about some sort of market. "I consider that a significant step towards financial stability would be to raise the interest rate of the Central Bank from 80% to 210%" - announced the then Minister of Finances B. Fedorov. Long term credit does not exist at all. So how are new enterprises supposed to be created and developed?

Financiers have a general rule that rates for bank credit have to be positive, (i.e. be higher than the rate of inflation). Then the players of the monetary market will lose interest in speculative monetary transactions, It also gives incentive for industrial investment.

Of course, the interest rate can not be separated from the inflation rate. But there are other, no less important, factors that affect a bank's lending rate, such as the financial balance of the enterprise, the amount of assets they own, the buffering policies of the government, the state of the government's balance of payments. Under our conditions these most important factors are not being studied or taken into account. So, having lowered the inflation rate in 1995 from 18% to 4-5%, the leadership was only able to lower the interest rate by 20% (from 200% to 160%).

Yeltsin – An Absolute Ruler

The exchange rate between the ruble and the dollar or other currency is beyond all rationale. Our national resources are being siphoned off into foreign countries because of the unjustifiably low rate of the ruble. Our domestic economy is just moving towards a market economy but, in the realm of foreign economic relations, we are jumping the gun and using a market exchange rate that is destructive to our economy. Western politicians will do anything to strengthen their country's national currency and to make it profitable in comparison to other currencies. The current currency rate of the ruble is drastically undervalued if we were to calculate it on the broadest comparable standard, the gross national product of Russia and of the United States. What do we hear from the Ministry of Finances: the low rate of the ruble promotes the export of goods. How one-sided! I worked in West Germany for six years and have witnessed the western economy under various conditions. In 1989, West Germany boldly increased the value of the deutsche mark. Prior to that, the social-democrat expert, Alex Miller, put together a list of pluses and minuses to changing the value of the currency. He came up with a couple dozen of them. Later Miller became the Minister of Finances and it was not surprising that he knew his business. Our monetary specialists only name one consequence of the devaluation of the ruble - it improves conditions for exporting goods. But at the same time import prices go up, the conditions for exporting capital deteriorate, etc. Russian monetary experts view the economy in linear terms, but economics is more complicated than that. Their achievements are not the result of real changes. For instance, they brought $2.5-$3 billion worth of credit back from the meeting of the Big Seven in Tokyo which was considered an achievement. But our own billions of dollars are lying in Russian banks and are not being used to develop the economy. Furthermore, billions of dollars from the profits of Russian enterprises' are annually transferred abroad where the money stays, because in Russia nobody cares about our own enterprises. Monetary specialists value a bank note more than they do goods and production.

Of course Yeltsin does not forget his devoted followers. Besides being loyal they have to execute his specific will. In important matters independence among lackeys is frowned upon.

One can frequently hear complaints about those surrounding Yeltsin. They are blamed for everything. They are the ones who give the President distorted information, the wrong advice, and they even force their own decisions upon him. Several tirades were made addressed against this "collective Rasputin." Of course, a lot does depend on one's subordinates.

Sometimes it does happen that the tail wags the dog, but this is not the case here. Even his closest aides are at risk of getting a scolding from their boss for any delays in executing his decrees. For instance, many in Yeltsin's circle advised him to create his own political party. This idea has been floating around since 1990. Prior to that it was not permissible to create parties. I will state, in order to note a historical truth, that in those days there were heated debates in the CPSU about Lenin's thesis on the inadmissibility of factions inside the party. By the time the thesis was confirmed yet another time, they discovered an even worse sin. While they were arguing about factions, new parties appeared in the country. At times it seemed that the idea of Yeltsin's party was about to become a reality. After all, he himself declared it publicly on a number of occasions. But Yeltsin decided against taking this decisive step at the last moment, rightfully anticipating the party would not be able to develop a solid foundation. Was this not an important independent decision?

The same thing happened once again before the elections during the Federal Meeting December 12, 1993, when Yeltsin decided formally against associating himself with the "Russia's Choice" block, which was headed by Gaidar. He did the right thing.

After the relative failure of the democrats during the Duma elections, Burbulis criticized the President's tactics. Yeltsin's political sense prompted him toward a strategy of victory, although he thinks that some-one is guiding him from above. This is one step away from mysticism, from that dangerous self-conceit about a divine purpose. Yeltsin, who is striving to take the position of the father of the nation, who unites the country, viciously revenged himself after the election against those who made miscalculations in the demo-cratic pre-election campaign. He did not even con-sider it necessary to explain his actions. Yeltsin acted in a like manner after the Duma election in 1995. The most vivid example is the firing of the Vice Premier Chubais. Yeltsin blamed him for the low results of the entire presidential and government contingent head-ed by V. Chernomyrdin ("Our Home Is Russia" - OHR). If it weren't for Chubais, Yeltsin said, OHR would have gotten 20% of the vote. Yeltsin determined this 20% figure based on the results of the elections in Moscow, where the business-like mayor, U. Luzhkov, successfully prevented Chubais from privatizing government enter-prises for a pittance. A question arises; where was Yeltsin himself before the elections? After all, Chubais was squandering valuable state property through pri-vatization and security auctions, which were approved by the President and the Premier. It is a rhetorical ques-tion, (i.e. as the answer is clear it does not need to be answered).At this point Yeltsin has 90% of the power in the country, and all the rest listed as leading politicians in Russia have 10%.

In terms of Yeltsin's associates and high ranking democrats in general, the following stares you in the face. We thought that these people were fighting for an idea, but instead they are fighting for their own profit. Yeltsin himself is not susceptible to avarice but he is lenient toward this vice in others and even takes advantage of it. The privileges of the former era, the fight against which brought him glory, were recreated and expanded for the new elite. I will even dare to say that Yeltsin's rise to power was aided by his taking advantage of the avarice of others. At the very peak of his fight against I. Polozkov for the position of Chairman of the Supreme Soviet of the RSFSR in 1990, at the Congress of Deputies Yeltsin proposed that deputies should be able to work in the Supreme Soviet in capacities other than the position to which they were elected. Elected officials heard this and saw it as a chance to penetrate a powerful structure, and out-of-towners saw an opportunity to plant themselves in Moscow. This tactical move provided Yeltsin votes, but it signified the creation of a new system of privileges for the new nomenclature. We thought that the democrats were fighting wholeheartedly for an idea, but it turned out that many of them primarily sought and continue to seek personal positions and financial benefits.

Consequently, the democrats would like to consider Yeltsin a constant patron. For some it worked, for some it did not. The dissatisfaction and even opposition stems from this. An incident with Gaidar is telling. As soon as he felt that Yeltsin's chances for being re-elected as president in June of 1996 were questionable, Gaidar, in January 1996, retreated from the midst of Yeltsin's supporters and called upon his colleagues to follow suit.

I evaluate this as an act of utter ingratitude on the part of Gaidar, who forgot to whom he owes everything (everything!). It is possible that Gaidar is guided in his actions by fear that the communists will come to power, and make him answer for his actions. But even that excuse does not change my evaluation of Gaidar's somersault.

To achieve his political goals Yeltsin significantly weakened Russia as a state. I am referring to his 1990 proposition directed at the autonomous regions - take as much freedom as you can swallow. This started a phase in which other territories were carried away with the idea of free economic zones.

It is a well known fact that the Soviet Union was marked by its extreme centralization in management. All regions were measured with one stick. Everything was taken out of the regions and redistributed. The local natural wealth did not make the local population wealthy. The Republic of Sakha (Yakutia) is rich with diamonds, but it was and is impoverished. The Magadan region is rich with gold, the Tyumen region is rich with oil, but the economic situation there was and remains difficult.

Towards the end of the existence of the Soviet Union, the regions began feeling the weakening of the Center and began a movement towards greater independence and tried to win the status of free economic zones (FEZ) for themselves.

The idea of creating FEZ, in the Soviet Union arose between the 80s and 90s under a planned system and the strong rule of the CPSU. It was still forbidden to discuss the introduction of a market economy, competition, private property, and a multi-party system in our country. The limit that you were allowed to write about was about commodity-monetary relations. Under these conditions the concept of FEZ, with references to positive experiences abroad was an attempt to break through the deceit of the command economy and the social system in general. It was a sort of Trojan horse with a pro-market filling. The relationship of the leaders of the USSR towards FEZ remained negative until the very end.

But when Yeltsin was fighting with Gorbachev, the leadership of the RSFSR became an interested supporter of FEZ. By taking this position they won over the leadership and the people of the regions that were fighting for a FEZ status. At that time, the local officials, had two main arguments in support of FEZ. Firstly, they pointed out that the given region was in a catastrophic situation and second, that Moscow had to grant significant economic and administrative privileges, which would force them either to go beyond the current law or to administer special acts. This argument was convincing in terms of the creation of FEZ. However, the main point was missed. The FEZ was being created, not for its own sake, no matter how impoverished it was, but to protect national interests. It had to become the extended arm of the government in the world market, and it had to work in a highly profitable and self-sufficient mode after the initial investment. Further, only those territories that have unique geographic locations that enable them to fulfill specialized tasks can become an FEZ. Yeltsin sanctioned the creation of a few FEZ but it was only a preliminary agreement. The final decision was to be made by the higher bodies of the USSR. After the dissolution of the USSR, when there was no more Gorbachev, and there was no more need to win over local administrators, the leadership of Russia drastically changed their position on FEZ. The leadership of FEZ, who were officially announced, had to listen to objections from the Russian government itself. These were the same familiar objections heard from the leadership of the USSR. Finally all the rulings concerning the creation of FEZ, were cancelled.

Yeltsin has also taken the following controversial step. The President of Russia appoints representatives who keep an eye on the regional governors and send written and oral reports to Moscow. The President's representative, by watching over the governor, unintentionally constrains his initiative. In the best of circumstances, these two appointees (most of the governors are appointed and only a few have been elected by the public) establish a good relationship and both work toward a market economy. But frequently this is not the case. During meetings with President Yeltsin, the Governors, constantly demanded the annulment of the institution of the President's representative, but without success. The President countered with the reply that the representatives supply him with the most reliable information. Yeltsin also promised his representatives to maintain this position in the regions as long as he is President of the country and he included this clause (provision) about his empowered representative in the Constitution of Russia.

A Paradox: Yeltsin is Antimarket

As a result of Yeltsin's ideological transformation from one extreme (Marxist-Leninist) to another (ideal-market), an extreme leftist perspective became prevalent if we were to start our calculation, with the ultra-right position of Nina Andreeva. V. Zhirinovsky does not fit on any scale. Any extremism is ruinous, as it obscures reason and is based on an unhealthy psychological foundation.

The current market educators are retrospectively seeking a basis for practical Yeltsinism in Western Economic Science. But they won't find it, because no serious scholar will defend monetarism in such an absurd form. In the meantime, the positions which were defended by the progressive branch of political economists toward the end of the Soviet period, have been given up. I will name two resolutions that pertain to our topic.

The first is that inflation is caused not simply by over filling cash flow channels with devaluated money, but by much deeper reasons related to the displacement of the entire societal production with huge disproportions inside the national economy. It would be naive to assume that by regulating the cash flow you can eliminate monopolism, the burdened industrial structure, the backwardness of agriculture and the entire assortment of negative traits in the country, that have accumulated in Russia's economy over the last seventy years.

The second resolution is that the law of manufacturing is higher than the law of cost. In other words, market relations cannot have preference a priory. They are only justified when they are instrumental in increasing industrial effectiveness. What the market cannot handle, the government must, and if there is no market, the government has to build one.

Not having adequate scholastic knowledge, nor practical experience, nor premature wisdom, the "young Turks" prefer chaos and ward off any attempts by others to explain to them the real state of affairs. Unfortunately because of this the movement toward a market economy is minimal. Continuing this reckless course will not achieve much. The bitter paradox is that Yeltsin's cabinet is playing a non-market, partially even an anti-market role, and has in itself become an obstacle to the movement towards a qualitatively new economy. We must come to realize this fact, although it is not easy to reach this truth due to the newly created stereotypical way of thinking: Yeltsin is considered a defender of market economy, and it is true that he was its instigator, but all of a sudden, when tested, he turns out to be anti-market in so far as his policies have not benefited the market.

You cannot create a market economy spontaneously. We cannot continue to have illusions on this account.

We do not need a managed economy on its own, but in order to support the vitality of the society and to build a market. The leap into a market economy and the resulting creation of an economic mess has yet another consequence - an increase in crime. It is a cancer infecting our society. If we were to take only the economic aspect, the evil brought about by the criminal structures is a hundred times worse than the infamous petty theft which was characteristic of the Soviet period. Corruption and organized crime have grown on such a broad scale that frequently the law enforcing units can only watch the events as they unfold.

Criminal groups are developing economic power. All the right conditions have been created for them in the economy and in society. Without the necessary state control and with undeveloped market relations, this third force, which has in many ways taken the place of the government and the market, was created and is rapidly overtaking new positions. The only thing it is lacking is an organizational unification and political legalization, but this is quite possible with further connivance of leadership.

But given all this, Yeltsin is not a lost case. In his Presidential Address in 1995, he used a series of phrasings that bear witness to the beginning of a positive process in his thinking. He is seconded by V. Chernomyrdin, who announced that the period of economic romanticism is over, monetarism did not prove itself. However, practical policies have not undergone any changes and the destruction of the economy continues. Sensible social forces must increase the pressure on higher administration. As Khrushchev liked to say, for everything there is a season. Well, this vegetable is ripe enough to understand that it is time to change our economic course before those below change those who are on the top.

The Russian Malady – What Will the West Say

One can rightfully ask: to whom does Yeltsin have to demonstrate his democratism? Who is grading him? The West is of course. The ideals of sovereignty of the people have not sunken in yet in our society. The people might very well confuse one definition with another, and they seem to miss a strong arm. But the West has experienced all fields of democracy, so that is where we need to consult. Especially since it is giving out credit. What a blessing that the West exists. Without it we never would be able to understand anything about universal values. But the West is not homogenous either. For instance, the famous American political analyst Z. Brzezinski announced in February of 1993 that the West should not have demanded quick economic changes from Russia. First the political system needs to be changed and strengthened. Someone might say: one witness is no witness. But Brzezinski is far from being alone in such opinions. But Yeltsin prefers to be guided by radicals both at home and abroad.

It would be natural after such an analysis to come to the conclusion that I am inciting against Yeltsin. No, that is not so. Life is more precarious than that. Churchill's comment that the democratic system is full of flaws, but still the best one there is, is applicable to our President. Fear a horse from behind, a goat from the front and a spry person on all sides - as the saying goes. We have learned a few things and know what to fear and what not to fear from Yeltsin. We know him and there is nothing new to find. We can read him like an open book. So regardless of all the accusations made about his Napoleonic tendencies, he remains a committed democrat. Besides these accusations are being invented by people, who given the chance would tightened the screws, just like in the old days. The dissolution of Parliament and the Congress of Peoples Deputies does not change anything in this definition [of him being a true democrat]. They both dropped so low in the eyes of society and -I am not afraid of using a beat up phrase here in the eyes of the world community, and they came so close to their cherished goal of illegally toppling the President, that the latter was forced to act in self defense at the very least. Even then, the actions Yeltsin took against the federal bodies in question were inadequate and soft, and it allowed the opposition to take up arms. And once again Yeltsin hesitated for a very long time before he made the decision to shoot directly at the White House from tanks. The storming of the White House signified putting a stop to the destruction of the Russian state. But shortly after, Yeltsin, himself, revived the instability, by signing the agreement between Moscow and Tatarstan and later with other regions of the Federation.

What is completely uncharacteristic of Yeltsin is giving warning signals. He is idle until he once again is convinced that he is trapped in somebody's net. So far he has been lucky. He has been able to escape. For instance, he is frequently reproached for not dissolving the Congress and the Soviets on all levels immediately after the August putsch of 1991. Those who accuse him are proving that they do not know Yeltsin at all. It is beyond his strength to break away from empiricism and to peek into the future. The accusation is also unfounded because after the coup, the Russian leadership attempted to unify. At that time, the Russian Federation was fighting for its independence from the USSR and Yeltsin had the support of the majority of the Republic's deputies. It was not at all necessary at the time to accelerate elections.

Yeltsin demonstrated his peaceable disposition which bordered on being carefree after the referendum April 25, 1993, when Yeltsin and his politicians received the peoples approval. Many Yeltsin experts, and almost all journalists consider themselves to be experts, lost a bet when they insisted that if Yeltsin won he would dismiss the people's deputies on April 27 (it was thought that on the 26th he would study the results of the election). Days passed, the victor studied the results of the election, but he never did bring himself to disperse the Congress and hold a re-election, although he had every right to do so. In this instance he acted more democratically than Western democrats.

On the Decline

A s the economic situation in the country deterio-rated further, Yeltsin's ratings declined. "Put Boris on the tracks," the signs demanded, referring to Yeltsin's promises to lie down on the railroad tracks if things did not improve. Some people's demands were even worse. Yeltsin was no doubt concerned by agitation among the people. But it is easier to under-stand it now. In the course of his transformation from being a pillar of the administrative-command system to becoming an adherent of a market economy, he went through yet another transformation. What we have before us now is not the severe party hack who without objecting followed Moscow's orders to destroy the house in which the czarist family had been exe-cuted, or who built the tallest building in Sverdlovsk for the regional Committee of the Communist Party. What we have now is a neophyte democratic, who instantly accepted all the values of the West.

When did he have the time? I write this not iron-ically, but with sincere approval. It would have been easier for him to live and work the old way, and I imag-ine he is sometimes overcome by nostalgia. But the new value system has strengthened itself in his mind and it can be altered. He holds the division of power sacred and if he does invade someone else's territo-ry, it is not out of spite, but to defend his own interests.

Like a black panther, he never starts the quarrel first, but he can really give a thrashing. He is a typical Russian bear. Once he shocked a lot of people, when during a speech at the House of Cinematography, when he urged that the enemy be fought not hugged - even if they are women.

He has already suffered because of his devotion to democracy. After being elected President, in the euphoria of victory, he turned down the leadership of the Congress of the Peoples Deputies. He could have maintained that position even had it meant amending the Constitution. He led the Congress brilliantly. He could have gotten a majority of those which counted to agree with his amendments. He was also a competent Chairman of the Supreme Soviet, yet he could not be called the Speaker of the House even in retrospect. What let him down was the mistaken belief that he could count on the continued support of both forums. It turned out that he was too rash in giving up his seat as chairman in the historic chamber of the Grand Kremlin Palace. That chamber is no more.

Logical differences at the top of our power structure created sharp political conflicts. On the one hand, the presidency was the highest position of power. On the other hand, the Congress of People's Deputies represented the highest body of power. Consequently whoever presided over the Congress, could challenge the President. It is no longer important why Yeltsin, as leader of the Congress, retracted his position—consciously or out of shortsightedness. What is done is done. Realizing this, Yeltsin made his plans for the future accordingly.

The former number two man in the Politburo, Egor Ligachev has expressed regrets for being too passive after the collapse of communism saying, "If it were to happen now, we would put up a fight." Even Mikhail Gorbachev, himself, if he were given a chance to do it all over, would not give up his power so easily and would not rely so much on pageantry.

Gorbachev's most critical mistake in his fateful fight with Yeltsin was that he underestimated the Congress of People's Deputies of Russia. While Yeltsin was on the ballot for the position of Chairman of the Supreme Soviet and Gorbachev flew to the USA to meet with Bush. Yeltsin won by a few votes. Had Gorbachev and the Central Committee functionaries had fully realized what was at stake here, they could have prevented such an insignificant majority in Yeltsin's favor. But the customary self-assuredness had an adverse effect on the General Secretary and other high-ranking party members. Gorbachev himself sometimes took his proper place in Congress, but he was more frequently absent. The members of the Central Committee would only associate with deputies who were from the Communist Party. They would meet with them, and even then it was mostly with first secretaries of regional and city committees. As for the Chairmen and deputies of the regional executive committees, they never saw hide nor hair of them, not to mention other elected representatives of the people. But then what was the Russian Federation in the USSR? A republic without rights. It was governed not by the Russian Federation's leaders (Vorotnikov and Vlasov at the time) but by the almighty Politburo of the Communist Party. Sizing up the prospects for the future, Gorbachev may have feared (but not much) that Yeltsin would take control of the Russian government. After all, Yeltsin's power was only nominal.

Politics can be amazing. For example someone in business were to lie so blatantly and the lie soon surfaced, it would lead to the demise of the company and the disgrace of the entrepreneur. A miscalculation of the same broad scope in science or engineering would lead to layoffs or demotions. But in politics— it is accepted. Within a year of making this claim Yeltsin became president. Those are the rules of the game: paying for your actions is not necessary. Even in this case, however, one might be able to excuse Yeltsin on the grounds that he was not just deceiving the people, he was also deceiving himself. He merely said what he believed. And why did he say it? Because he wanted to lead Russia. First nominally and later in the future, we will have to see. You cannot punish someone for his aspirations.

The Opposition Was Even Worse

A few words should be said about Yeltsin's opposition. At one point they had a rational basis, manifested in their criticism of Yeltsin's reform plans—in their call to redirect reform into an evolutionary course, thereby avoiding a forced destruction of the economic apparatus, and an abrupt dismantling of established industrial ties. A lot of good things could be said about this rational basis, but I for one continue to be skeptical of their true intentions: did they ever truly support a free market economy?

It is possible that Yeltsin's opponents were only hiding behind market phraseology, and even then one could see through to their true Soviet nature. But let us suppose that they really did transform into promarketeers, who differed from Yeltsin not in their end goals, but in the means for realizing them. What would have happened if Yeltsin had shown solidarity with the People's Deputies' right-wing faction regarding the means of carrying out reform? He would have been criticized by the left for not being decisive in his actions, and the right would still have tried to remove him in order to assume power.

Yeltsin's harmony with his "lieutenants," whom he, himself chose and placed but one rung below himself, lasted for eight to nine months. While they were adapting to their new positions and unexpected wealth and power, they conducted themselves properly. After they had become accustomed to their positions they began to covet Yeltsin's power, though they were not mentally fit for his position. Yeltsin, with his natural generosity, initially did not react adequately to the independent steps and tricks of his closest aides. He thought it was just their need for self-affirmation. By the time he realized that there was a serious threat, it was already impossible to rid himself peacefully of the "snake" coiled on his chest. If they had been victorious they would have held on to power as tenaciously as they had opposed Yeltsin. Like the Bolsheviks, they would not have parted with their power voluntarily.

Nobody forced Yeltsin to carry out the April, 1991 vote of confidence that had seemed so catastrophic to his opponents. Yeltsin was also ready to move up the election to June, 1994. This demonstrates, not so much a love of risk, as zealous adherence to democracy, typical of the newly converted, and insecurity.

Even if the opposition initially had the right idea, they later compromised themselves through their gross violation of rights and by cynically scrambling for more power. They lost sight of their ideal. Yeltsin was bad enough, but his opponents were even worse.

The former People's Deputy, O. Rumiantsev published a curious and unexpected document, dated October 3, 1993, which appeared later in Pravda on September 21, 1995. It was a draft of the decree by

Acting President, A. Rutskoy, entitled "On the Appointment of Members to the Transitional Government of the Russian Federation." On the eve of the storming of the White House on October 3, deputies and experts compiled a list by candlelight of the coalition government headed by U. Skokov. At that time, I had been the Deputy Minister of Economy for a number of months. I was listed for the post of the Minister of Economy. Nobody asked for my approval on this appointment, nor were several other listed candidates asked. It is hard to judge how viable and effective the appointed transitional government would have been under those circumstances.

Just like the opposition to the President in 1993, Yeltsin's current opponents lack a strong leader. They have no reliable statesman capable of competing against Yeltsin for the Russian presidency. The elections for the state Duma on December 17, 1995, illustrated the lack of popularity of the multitude of power-hungry politicians. Their voting associations and blocs were unable to achieve the 5% minimum. Despite their obvious lack of popular support, they immediately got in line to run for president.

From the Kremlin to the Court – Is One Step

We know Yeltsin. But many other candidates for the country's highest post are wrapped in a veil of mystery. They have not gone through a trial run by working in an independent government post. The experience of the past three years has shown us what leaping into the realm of power without having any prior public responsibilities can lead to. It was a bitter experience. If we do not learn from this experience we will be forced to learn from our mistakes. Conditions are bad under Yeltsin, but without him, they could be a lot worse.

In contrast to the many other political figures incapable of hiding their overwhelming desire to lead Russia who, have, rushed to throw their hats in the ring, Yeltsin followed the rules of political diplomacy. He waited until February of 1996, to declare his candidacy for re-election. Of course, one could hardly doubt that he would run for a second term.

From ancient times, we can only cite a few examples of a person voluntarily refusing power, the most powerful narcotic. What is the sense in giving up the scepter that he fought so hard to win, the scepter that practically became his personal trophy. Especially since there is no guarantee that it will not fall out of the hand of his successor. In the second place, and here I repeat my own old thought, which you should, take as a warning, that Yeltsin's departure from his post may pose a threat to him. Active and nascent orthodox Bolsheviks would drag him through the courts (at the least) for the disintegration of the Soviet Union. So, he needs to hold on to the Kremlin at least for the sake of his personal safety.

The disappearance of the USSR is one of those rare occasions where in which with time the feelings of longing and pain do not disappear over the course of time, but rather intensify. At least in Russia. The anniversary of the demise of the Great Power is marked by the people as a day of mourning. Time transforms the August days of 1991 from the realm of an ordinary personal struggle for power to the realm of an epic struggle. It was the last battle for the last empire. The USSR is now a part of history. In my opinion, this empire was destined to collapse for two reasons. First, because it was built on violence; and secondly, because it opposed democracy as a concept of the West. If the forces opposing the Soviet Union were to have had the same dictatorial structure as its opposition, or if the Soviet Union were left to its own devises, it might have been able to exist eternally. But what left a deep wound was not the fact that the USSR fell into oblivion, but how this fall happened. The greatness of leaders is not measured by violence (Marx was right in his definition of violence as the midwife of history). Greatness is measured by how much the leaders promoted the prosperity of the country and its people; how much they enabled the national richness to increase under peaceful conditions and with social stability. If we were to apply this measurement to political figures in the Soviet Union and Russia, they would measure smaller than the events. Thus, Yeltsin and Gorbachev were in a way competing with each other: who will grant freedom to the Baltic Republics first. They gave it to them. And only after the fact, did they try to initiate negotiations with the Baltic Republics and, naturally, were refused. Latvia, Lithuania and Estonia did not accept the conditions that were being offered.

The results of the disintegration of the Great Power turned out to be extremely grave. The Russian people are experiencing a tragedy of historic proportions. If they suffered while they were a part of the Soviet Union just as the other people did, and they did not act as a hegemonic Nation, now they are torn apart. Twenty-five million Russian people have been left to their fate beyond the borders of Russia. Many of them are being discriminated against because of their nationality and are forced to struggle for their survival.

The collapse of the Soviet Union is interpreted by Yeltsin's opposition, similar to the results at the Belovezh Puscha [forest], as an act of treason. And Yeltsin will have to answer this grave accusation if he lets go of the reins of power. Whether he was right or not from a historical point of view is irrelevant. That is also typical of the genre of politics.

The Southern Kuril Islands

In January of 1990, Boris Yeltsin visited Japan. While he was there he announced his five-stage plan for resolving the territorial dispute with Japan over the Southern Kurils. At the time, Yeltsin was not the official leader and was Gorbachev's main opponent in the struggle for power. Yeltsin made two grave mistakes then. He admitted that the territorial problem existed and did not exclude the possibility of giving the islands to Japan depending on the situation on the islands and on the relationship between the countries. Thus, he laid the groundwork for Gorbachev who, during his visit to Japan in April of 1991, also admitted that the territorial problem existed. Gorbachev then deviated the Soviet-Japanese Declaration from 1956 and added two more islands to those in dispute. I happened to be in Tokyo during Gorbachev's visit. But having felt the capitulating tendencies of the Soviet president and of his closest advisors, I expressed my misgivings to the high-level delegation on the second day, and flew back to Moscow.

The topic of the Kuril Islands has undermined relations between Russia (and previously the Soviet Union) and Japan. The essence of the dispute is that Japan has claims on these islands: Etorufu, Kunashiri, Shikotan, and a group of small islands called Habomai, which were occupied by the USSR at the end of Second

World War. The territory of the islands adds up to around ten thousand square kilometers, but this figure rises to two hundred thousand square kilometers when the turn around waters are taken into account.

Soviet forces attached the Kurils on September 1, 1945, and on September 2, Japan surrendered unconditionally.

Having sensed the possibility of a favorable settlement to the Northern Territories Japan has increased the pressure on Moscow over the last few years.

Having sensed the possibility of a favorable settlement to the Northern Territories on Moscow having sensed the possibility of successfully resolving the Northern territories conundrum.

Russia does not have a "territorial problem." The Southern Kuril Islands are neither burdensome nor insignificant territory for us. They have an economic and geopolitical significance. This is precisely why Japan is so insistent on possessing them.

A problem does exist, however, for our neighbors across the La Perouse Strait. However this does not mean that we need to share in it. It is impossible to ignore completely the Japanese question, because we want to develop a friendly relationship with that country. I myself am an avid supporter of this position. Japan, a great economic empire, is now flaunting its miraculous technology and sacks of money to a Russian government in crisis. Tokyo has offered to exchange the disputed territories in exchange for Japanese assistance, without specifying what form this assistance would take. And why should they specify anything when our leaders, captivated by Japanese power, and hoping to get at least some scraps from the royal table, are warming up to the thought of handing over (that is, selling) these four barren rocks. But selling territory that belongs to the people is not the final stage of political and moral disintegration. Others have hit rock bottom: for reasons only known to them, they are ready not only to give away the islands for nothing, but are also to beg forgiveness for the delay in doing so. It is thought that Japan will take Russia's atonement into consideration in determining economic policy towards our country.

Our politicians are clearly buckling under Japan's pressure and are putting the territorial dispute on the agenda of the Russian government.

The very awkwardness of the situation is demonstrated by the fact that Russian politicians in official positions capitulated to a foreign power, when they ordered embassy personnel to treat the Southern Kuril Islands differently than Russia.

Tokyo is pressuring not only Moscow, but other capitals as well, in an attempt to internationalize the problem. This tactic has borne some fruit. A number of countries support Japan's demands, again out of mercantile interests. An economic giant can show its benevolence to those who share their outlook on this issue, whereas those who do not support its policies must accept the consequences.

There are hundreds of disputed islands in the world. But the same countries that take the Southern Kuril problem to heart show little or no interest in these other disputes. What we are dealing with is the selective execution of justice on the world stage.

There is another example that is relevant to the current discussion. The former Prime Minister of England, Margaret Thatcher, engaged Britain on an armed conflict over the question of her democratic convictions. "One of us will not survive this confrontation" she declared, with the Argentinean President General Galtieri in mind. She won, and her opponent not only lost his office, but also ended up in prison.

From time immemorial, the shape of national borders has been determined by strength. But "strength" may take many different forms. Currently, the most important form is economic strength and Russia is feeling its effects along its remotest borders. If we neglect our interests there, we shall be forced to give up other Russian regions as well. Russian politicians have yet to realize the connection between economics and politics in international affairs. So far they are simply reacting to events and in so doing frequently go against national interests. But it is imperative they be able to foresee the development of events and shape them in a way that is beneficial to the country.

The new political thinking established in our country includes the rejection of the former stereotypes of Soviet politics, aggressive tactics on the international stage and attempts to interpret historical facts in our favor a priory. We should support the new doctrine in any way possible. But does this imply a "one way street?" I think not. Our international partners also have to be subjected to this new way of thinking. In the meantime, territorial demands are nothing more than a holdover from the past, and, as such, are potentially aggressive acts.

The policy of elbowing one's way to the redrafting of new borders should be considered to be outdated and unconstructive in our era. Historical references cannot serve as a convincing argument, since the territories in question may well have belonged to both sides at different times in history. And the concept of sovereignty is often interpreted in different, and even contradictory ways by the parties involved.

The scope of Japanese propaganda on the Kuril question is illustrated by the following facts: the Japanese Parliament has repeatedly issued resolutions demanding the return of the territories; the same demands have been made at prefecture-, city-, and village-level meetings throughout the country; tens of millions of signatures have been collected supporting the return of the Kurils; every prefecture of Japan has created so-called "Civil Councils for the Return of the Northern Territories."

Since 1981, February 7th, has been marked as the "Day of the Northern Territories." (February 7th, 1855 is the day when the Russo-Japanese treaty was signed, under the terms of which Japan acquired the disputed islands). It must be noted that currently there are no Japanese living on the Southern Kuril Islands, whereas in 1945 there were sixteen thousand. Along the expressways of the northern Japanese island of Hokkaido there are billboards devoted to the territorial issue. The disputed islands are drawn as the same color as Japan on political maps. The Japanese government stresses their unwavering opposition to Japanese citizens visiting the disputed islands. Such trips, which require obtaining a Russian visa, are viewed as in legitimizing the continuing occupation of the islands.

The Japanese government is also very vocal on the international stage on this issue. I will give only one example. The Japanese embassy in West Germany sent the following notice to German companies at the end of 1992: "Japan repudiates all such actions on the four Kuril Islands that substantiate Russian claims on these islands. Such actions work against the long-standing efforts of the Japanese people to resolve this territorial issue. In the event that the Kuril Islands are restored to Japan, the commercial interests created through such activities will not be considered legitimate under Japanese law. We therefore urge you to put an end to such activities." The Japanese continue to stress that a necessary condition for friendly relations based on true mutual understanding with Russia is the settling of the issue of the Northern Territories.

In the Soviet-Japanese Peace Declaration of October 19, 1956, our country agreed to give Japan the islands of Habomai and Shikotan on the condition that the Soviet Union actually "hand over" the islands upon the signing of a non-aggression pact with Japan. The irreconcilability of the two countries' positions prompted the Soviet government to abandon this condition.

On January 27, 1960, an official memorandum from the Soviet to the Japanese government stated: "On January nineteenth of this year, the so-called "Agreement on Mutual Cooperation and Safety" was signed by Japan and the USA. The content of this agreement touches in no small measure upon the situation in the Far East and the Pacific Basin, and thus upon the interests of many countries located in this vast region, especially the direct neighbors of Japan, the Soviet Union and the Peoples Republic of China. . . In agreeing to surrender to Japan the islands in question upon signing of a non-aggression pact, the Soviet government complied with Japanese demands in accordance with the two nations' interests and peaceful intentions, which were expressed by the Japanese government in the course of Soviet-Japanese negotiations. However, the new military agreement signed by Japan and the USA is aimed against the Soviet Union as well as against the Peoples Republic of China. The Soviet government cannot now surrender the Kurils to Japan if such action would result in territory being occupied by foreign troops. In view of this, the Soviet Government is obligated to declare that the islands Hobomai and Shikotan will be given to Japan per the mutual declaration of October 19, 1956, only in such case that all foreign troops will be removed from Japan, and that a non-aggression pact between the USSR and Japan is signed."

On February 24, 1960, the Japanese government received yet another significant memorandum from the Soviet government which stated: "By signing the Military Agreement with the USA, which is aimed against the security of the Soviet Union, Japan has obviously violated its commitment to cooperate with the Soviet Union in the interests of peace and security in the Far East. To establish friendly relations between the two countries as set forth in the mutual declaration. Therefore, we can only be surprised at the current attempts of the Japanese government to the blame the Soviet Union for violating the conditions of the non-aggression pact. In reality, the fulfillment of the conditions of the Soviet-Japanese Declaration of 1956, which Japan itself violated, depends solely on the Japanese government."

Thus, there was a chance to resolve the Kurils question, but it was missed. Now we need to find new approaches to this issue. Everybody who touches the topic of territorial disputes should be aware of this necessity, and they should present documents and quotes from their historical context. Life does not stand still. It creates new realities. Political wisdom should be measured by the ability to find current answers to contemporary issues, not try to destroy a new reality by returning to an old one.

The hopes of the Japanese to take advantage of Russia's immoral role in certain events (for example, the declaration of war on Japan despite a non-aggression pact) cannot be fully justified. All participants of high-level politics are tainted: Japan, became itself, by plundering the Asian-Atlantic region and annexing it for sometime, as well as our former allies, who promised the Soviet Union territorial gains if it entered into the war against Japan.

Let us be cold-blooded and assume that Russia would receive billions of dollars for the islands. That would be a drop of fresh water in the saltwater sea of our problems. Our inefficient system will consume the money, and in a couple of years Russia will have neither money nor islands. The conclusion is obvious: we need to change our economic system; then we will have our own millions. The waters off the Southern Kuril Islands are so rich with natural resources that the change of ownership would drastically disadvantage the national economic potential of Russia. The islands will strengthen Japan's power, whereas Russia will never be able to compensate for the huge economic loss. Its eastern flank will be strategically undermined.

Japan's statements about aiding the development of Siberia and the Far East if they get the territories should be treated as fairy tales. Private capital has never wanted to engage in any activity that is not profitable. Japan would offer us more government credit, and this has many positive sides. But there is one drawback: it has to be paid back with interest. That means new debts when we are already drowning in the ones we have. Why is it better to become indebted to Japan than to another country? What can Japan offer us that is more profitable than the goods, services and conditions already available in the world market?

The answer was already given by another country— The Federal Republic of Germany. The toothless concession of the Soviet Union that allowed West Germany to consume East Germany in a matter of months has few analogies in world history. And what became of it? German capital is not intended to eliminate our economic ruin and no one can force them to.

To return to the Kuril question, Japanese capital is directed toward those in branches of the economy that are profitable, regardless of any territorial dispute. The Japanese compete with foreigners for market share in the areas which they want to do business with Russia. Japan's cultivation of the very rich Sakhalin shelf in order to extract oil and gas is an example. Japanese cities even compete with each other for economic agreements with Sakhalin's populated areas.

By weakening the status of the Southern Kuril Islands as Russian territory we are sowing seeds which will grow into serious problems for future generations. We need to recognize that if this problem that is being forced on us is not resolved to our satisfaction, then the two-sided relationship will be marked by rancor—only this time on the Russian side. Then how sorry we shall be, my dear reader! After the lessons of Alaska, Port Arthur, and the Chinese-Eastern Railroad we cannot allow this to happen.

I must say that I consider the polls of the opinions of inhabitants of Sakhalin and the Kurils regarding the fate of these islands to be completely unnecessary. This is not because they prove what is already known - i.e., that the overwhelming majority of these inhabitants are in favor of remaining part of Russia - but rather because by conducting them we are expressing doubt in the strength of our position. Polls are conducted when something is not clear. There is no lack of clarity in the issue of the Southern Kuril Islands. We should not weaken our own position. We should not give our partners the impression that we are confused or unsure. And what if tomorrow they demand South Sakhalin from us, and then all of Sakhalin, all of the Kuril Islands or regions of Siberia? Will we poll the residents of those areas as well?

After all, Japan's definition of its "Northern Territories" is not limited to the Kurils.

Betrayal has always played a part in history. In every era baseness of character and self-interest are at the root of betrayal and, alas, betrayal is alive and well in international politics. While I was the Governor of Sakhalin and the Kurils, I came directly into contact with the "fifth column", in Moscow whose position is one hundred percent Japanese. They use the same anti-Russian arguments that Japanese politicians do without subjecting them to any critical analysis. Thus, the plot was being conceived by those close to the Russian throne. I could rely on no one. The double dealers said one thing to my face, while behind my back they would be kowtowing to the Japanese establishment.

There is no question among Russians about to whom the islands belong. The politicians who want to oblige the Japanese understand this. In the beginning of the 1990s they began a lengthy assault on popular opinion. Their goal was to 'enlighten' the ignorant Russian people in the hopes that the result of such a campaign would be the people's agreement to the demands of Tokyo. The destabilization and collapse of the USSR inspired the adherents of this course of action. The Japanese also became more animated. In the past they had posed the question of the sovereignty of the Kurils very timidly. Arguments about historical justice were rightly swept aside by the Soviets. The Governor of Hokkaido told me that one of the leaders of the Russian Federation at the time, V. Vorotnikov, had denied the existence of the territorial question entirely. With time our leaders softened, however, especially during their visits to Japan. Rarely were they able to maintain Russian prestige during their visits. Why? Either they had no backbone or they were 'bribed' with money or gifts. Whatever the cause, among part of the Russian leadership there is now a conspiracy at work against the South Kurils. Latishev named these conspirators in his two books about the islands.

The nerve center of the conspiracy turned out to be the Russian Ministry of Foreign Affairs under Minister Andrei Kozyrev. He selected personnel who agreed with his own positions to work on the Kuril question. What have we come to when the departments that are entrusted with protecting the national interest play right into the hands of foreign countries? The deputy minister, G. Kunadze, particularly excelled at this. Visiting Sakhalin during my tenure as Governor, he announced to everyone in no uncertain terms that the fate of two of the four islands had already been decided, that they would be given to the Japanese. The fate of the other two was left uncertain, but he implied that they might also be returned to Japan.

In the December 5, 1995 issue of "Pravda" there was an article published by a Mr. Arin entitled "The Anatomy of a Bribe". He writes: "I myself was especially zealous when I was serving as director of one of the small institutes in Vladivostok. In the media I called for the transferal of the Northern territories to Japan. Other Japanese specialists who also favored such a transferal showed more restraint, (one of them was in the Ministry of Foreign Affairs [Kunadze—VF]), but essentially they were writing and saying the same things. At the time, all of us, especially the representative of the Ministry of Foreign Affairs, were attacked by the Governor of Sakhalin, Valentin Fedorov. At that time, I did not understand him at all: how could the USSR claim these lands that had never belonged to Russia? 'So what?' Fedorov responded. 'Many places were annexed during the Second World War. What of it? Territories have been occupied throughout history. The islands are ours. Period.' Only now, after carefully studying the history of the USA, do I understand that his words make a lot of sense. For some reason it does not occur to a single American to return territories that the United States occupied by force."

Mr. Arin raises the possibility that members of the political-academic establishment "sold out" and mentions specifically the Institute of World Economy and International Relations, where I worked for twenty-one years, and the Institute of the USA and Canada. As a professor and later as Governor, I came to know this establishment from the inside, and I accuse our self-appointed intellectual leaders of betraying the interests of Russia on the Southern Kurils question.

Mr. Arin deserves credit for his courage in admitting that he was bribed and telling his Russian colleagues (whom he calls "reptilians") that they are also being bribed. Once, after one of the "capitulation sessions" in Moscow, I flew to the capital to participate in an important meeting at the Kremlin. During the break I resolutely headed over to Yeltsin. As soon as he saw me he began repeating, "Please keep calm! Please keep calm!" I have had the opportunity to speak to Yeltsin about the Southern Kurils on more than one occasion and have formed the impression that he has departed from his earlier mistaken position.

Even among the Japanese themselves, the issue is not so clear-cut. A part of the population does not agree with the official demands of Tokyo. The leader of the Ainu people, who lives on Hokkaido, has discussed the Kuril question with me several times, and I have come to the conclusion that these people do not see eye to eye with Japanese politicians. Incidentally, in the archives of South Sakhalin is recorded a historical fact that the employees of the Ministry of

Foreign Affairs should keep in mind: the indigenous people of the Kuril islands paid taxes to the Czar and accepted his leadership.

The Japanese policy of isolation from the rest of the world lasted for over two centuries. The Japanese authorities would not even let back into the country fishermen who had been aided by foreign vessels when their ships were wrecked. This slowed down Japan's' drive to the Kurils and Sakhalin, when the Cossacks and other Russians were developing the west and north parts of the region.

It is not my intention to make the extreme claim that the Kurils have always belonged to Russia. However, by the same token, they have not always belonged to Japan. History, in fact, is on the Russian side. But history is not even as important as the current sate of affairs. The wars for territory in the former Soviet Union should instruct us all, including Japanese politicians, about the value of the status quo. Territorial restoration will lead to grave consequences for Japan itself. Of course, now there is a movement afoot to return the Northern territories (which include, in the extremist view, both the Kurils and Sakhalin). But such restoration would provoke a movement in Russia to re-annex the Northern Territories—one much larger in scope and more dangerous for the fate of the world. No, it is best to leave the Kurils undisturbed.

There are no Japanese there at all now. Why is this? The Minister of Foreign Affairs omits important facts in answering to this question. He does not even question the Japanese version of history, which states that the Russians forced the Japanese population out. Incidentally, the condition of the Ainu people, who were forced out earlier and are now unsatisfied with how Japan is treating them, is completely lost in the argument for the 'human right' of the Japanese population on the Kurils. Returning to the year 1945, the Emperor signed a decree at the end of the war stating that all Japanese subjects must return to their land. There is more to this decree than meets the eye: the American military command did not want the USSR to appear as its partner in defeating Japan. It was they who insisted that Tokyo recall all Japanese from the Kurils; otherwise, these islands would have been seen as Japanese territory captured by the Soviet Union. The Americans thus killed two birds with one stone: they avenged the insult of Pearl Harbor, and they fulfilled their promise to 'give' the Kurils to the Soviet Union on the condition that it take part in the war in the Pacific.

In the fall of 1990, after Yeltsin visited Kunashir and me, he publicly announced that he had been mistaken in considering the Southern Kuril Islands "bare rocks," and that Russia could not cede their riches to another country. Nevertheless, Yeltsin did not put an end to the unseemly actions of the Ministry of Foreign Affairs. A weakening in the Russian military presence in the Kurils could have grave consequences. The small number of well-equipped and disciplined troops that are stationed there maintain the vitality of the islands, which in their absence would be abandoned because of the trying natural conditions (hurricanes, snowstorms, earthquakes). Thus, we should not ignore the real possibility of a 'peaceful takeover' by Japanese extremists.

Over the past years of economic transition, one very change has occurred in the attitude of our leadership. They (and this includes Yeltsin) now understand that no amount of foreign aid will close the gaps in our economy. The illusion of a quick walk down the path of reform arm in arm with a foreign banker in his top hat and cane has been dissolved. There is one more task left: we must understand that giving up the Southern Kurils will lead to great economic damage to Russia due to the loss of several billion dollars worth of revenue from sea products every year This sum is far greater than that which Japan can hope to offer in exchange for these 'bare rocks.' In reality, the Southern Kurils are a treasure trove that has not been fully exploited for the benefit of Russia.

At my insistence, Yeltsin on December 8, 1992, signed a decree "On the Socio-Economic Development of the Kuril Islands." In it, the Kurils were declared a special economic zone and were granted significant economic privileges. However, after I departed from Sakhalin in April 1993, this decree — like so many others — was left to wither on the vine. Incidentally, the document was signed on the last day of Yeltsin's 'expanded powers' — November 30, 1992. On December 1, the regular session of the Congress of Peoples' Deputies was opened and these special powers were abrogated. Prior to this date, presidential decrees had been reviewed by the Supreme Soviet for one week. Then, barring any objections, the latter would return the dated decrees to Yeltsin, at which point they would become law. After Gaidar, his cabinet, and I had agreed on the final corrections to the draft of the Kuril Islands Decree, days passed and no further action was taken. It was only after I wrote a strident communique, (the tone was entirely appropriate under the circumstances,) that the decree was finally signed. This law is still in force and should be followed to the letter.

We should strongly fault Prime Minister Chernomyrdin. In the fall of 1993, after returning from a visit to the Kurils he publicly declared that Russia would not allow the islands to starve and that it was capable of feeding their ten thousand people. (Why he settled on this figure is a mystery to me, since the population of the Kurils is some twenty-five thousand.) The Prime Minister received a round of applause then. Since that time, however, nothing has been done. It is most ironic that Tokyo allots the island of Hokkaido a large sum from the national budget for the development of the Southern Kurils when the islands do not even belong to it. The government of Sakhalin on the other hand, in whose jurisdiction the islands do fall, does not receive anywhere near the funds necessary for their maintenance. As a result, the inhabitants of these long suffering 'bare rocks' are leaving in large numbers. The Southern Kurils have been abandoned by Moscow and, as a result were utterly unprepared for the 1994 earthquake.

As Governor, I was instrumental in creating among Russians a strong sense of the geophysical link between Russia and the Southern Kurils and did my utmost to insure that allegiance to the islands be seen by Russians as a matter of patriotism and national pride.

DECREE OF THE PRESIDENT OF THE RUSSIAN FEDERATION

*on the socio-economic development
of the Kuril Islands*

In order to assure socio-economic stability and to strengthen the social protection of the population of the Northern Kuril, Kuril and Southern Kuril, areas of the Sakhalin District; in order to activate their economic development by utilizing all their natural recourses; to attract domestic and foreign investment; to broaden foreign economic activities; and also, in accordance to Resolution #13343-1 of the Presidium of the Supreme Soviet of the RSFSR of May 27, 1991, "On the Creation of the Sakhalin Free Economic Zone (Sakhalin FEZ), I hereby decree that:

1. The territories within the administrative boundaries of the Northern Kuril, Kuril, and Southern Kuril areas of the Sakhalin District shall be considered a special economic zone ('the Kurils') which shall function within the boundaries of the Sakhalin FEZ.

2. The following privileges shall be granted to enterprises and organizations, regardless of their legal organization, duly registered on the territory of the Northern Kuril, Kuril, or Southern Kuril areas of the Sakhalin District:

a. the independent utilization of the products they produce, including export, offshore and border sales. The export of said products shall be authorized by the Ministry of Foreign Economic Relations of the Russian Federation in the Sakhalin District to imploy accelerated amortization rates to all fixed assets as calculated by the administration of the Sakhalin District.

b. a waiver of the requirement that foreign currency proceeds from the sales of goods and services produced by manufacturers and the aforementioned organizations on the territory of the Kuril Islands be sold on the domestic market. In addition, exporting companies shall sell twenty percent of the foreign currency proceeds from the export of said goods and services to the currency fund for the development of said regions via authorized banks at the market exchange rate as per the regulations of the Central Bank of the Russian Federation.

3. In order to remove as many administrative, commercial, financial and other restraints on the development of the Northern Kuril, Kuril and Southern Kuril regions:

a. monetary (including foreign currency) funds received from the sales of licenses to foreign companies, Russian business and joint ventures, as well as revenue received as a result of inter-governmental agreements granting fish and other sea product catch rights in the Kuril fishing area of the Free Economic Zone of the Russian Federation, shall be allotted to the budgets and currency funds of the Northern Kuril, Kuril, and Southern Kuril regions to be used by the administration of said regions for the financing of priority works, including fishing agencies' maintenance of stock replenishment;

b. fines and compensation shall be collected in accordance with established rules for environmental degradation for breaking Russian fishing law, as well as for the depletion of fish stocks by other branches of industry, and shall be allocated to the budgets of the respective regions of the Kuril Islands to be used for the development of a material and technical base for marine protection agencies and for the border patrol;

c. the administration of the Sakhalin District shall have the right to determine independently catch limits for fish and other sea products in the Kuril fishing zone;

d. the administrative property committees of the Sakhalin, Northern Kuril, and Southern

Kuril regions shall have the right to sell government and municipal property to those parties chosen by the respective administrations. All revenue received from privatizing governmental assets shall be allotted to the non-budgetary accounts of said regions opened under Edict No.548 of the President of the Russian Federation of June 4, 1992, "On Proceedings To Develop Free Economic Zones on the Territory of the Russian Federation;"

e. the Council of Peoples' Deputies of the Northern Kuril, Kuril, and Southern Kuril regions shall be awarded the right to lease land to foreign investors for up to ninety-nine years.

4. The Government of the Russian Federation shall:

a. in formulating the government investment program for 1993-1995, provide funds for the construction and renovation of airports, roads, and engineering projects; the development of sea transportation and other means of communication; and the construction of ports as specified by the administration of the Sakhalin District;

b. in formulating the budget for the republics of the Russian Federation for 1993-1995, provide funds to the Ministry of Defense of the Russian Federation for the purposes of financing expenses connected with satisfying the social needs of the enlisted men and their families currently residing on the territory of the Northern Kuril, Kuril, and Southern Kuril areas of the Sakhalin District;

c. resolve the issue concerning the retraction of export duty on goods produced on the territory of said regions and the retraction of import duties on goods brought in for personal use.

5. The Government of the Russian Federation shall address the Supreme Soviet of the Russian Federation with the following proposals:

a. that revenue used for the financing, upkeep, and development of the socio-economic infrastructure or the agricultural-industrial complex on the territory of the Kuril Islands, as well as for technical renovations and reconstruction of enterprises authorized by local self-governing administrative bodies shall be free from taxes;

b. value added tax and excise monies, collected in accordance with the laws of the Russian Federation by enterprises and organizations registered in accordance with the regulations and engaged in the economy of the

Northern Kuril, Kuril, and Southern Kuril Region of the Sakhalin District shall be transferred to the local budgets of said areas.

6. This Decree shall not substantively alter the status of the Kuril Islands as part of the territory in the Sakhalin District of the Russian Federation.

7. By the Resolution "On the Legal Realization of Economic Reforms" of the Fifth Congress of the Peoples' Deputies of the RSFSR, this Decree shall be effective as of November 1, 1991.

President
Of the Russian Federation Boris Yeltsin

Moscow, The Kremlin
December 8, 1992
No.1549

Yeltsin's Decrees

Like horseshoes he forges decree after decree
Some get it in the groin, some in the head, some in the brow,
some in the eye.
O. Mandelshtam, 1933

The prominent German industrialist, Fritz Thiessen, actively helped Hitler come to power. He later became disillusioned with Hitler and escaped abroad, where he published a book entitled "I Paid Hitler," in which he showed the whole sordid truth. The book's publisher wrote in the preface about how Thiessen, when recalling the past, would grab his head with his hands and exclaim with remorse: "I was such an idiot!" This book continues to be of great interest to this day.

Now many people are grabbing their heads at the mention of Yeltsin's name. He himself describes some of his former cohorts in bleak tones. But we should not, however, expect him to express remorse for appointing his protege, Yegor Gaidar, who derailed the Russian economy in 1992. In the President's notes about the second Yegor (the first one is Ligachev) he expresses kind words. Neither will we hear a forthright confession that the government was mistaken in choosing an economic course in which market reforms were slated to begin and end within six to eight months.

Our President has a custom of addressing the people to ask for support and protection. In the beginning this played to the pride of many people. After decades of the Red Dictatorship's suppression of individuality, suddenly a leader is putting his fate in the hands of ordinary people. This device no longer works. Now the people have begun to ask - what is the President doing to protect us? And they answer themselves - nothing. He has broken promise after promise.

If we are to understand the economy as a system of interrelationships, then we must admit that Russia has no economy. There are enterprises that have been broken up after being released from government control. There are also new market structures that are trying to break through various administrative and financial barriers. Instead of helping the economy overcome a crisis, as is typically done for market economies in the West, our government has taken the stand of non-interference. It is acting in accordance with long outmoded scientific principles.

The economic edicts of the President demonstrate the experience that he has gained lately. He shall be blinded who forgets the past. Some of Yeltsin's orders radically contradict his own opinions expressed in the early stages of his presidency. Russia had to hit rock bottom before the control mechanisms, commonly used in other countries, were finally adopted. In the new Russia, free market opportunists considered these mechanisms to be heresy. By the same token, if Gaidar now praises Yeltsin's decrees on returning order, then he is following in the footsteps of his former boss, appearing before us unclothed, reminiscent of the fairy tale about the emperor's new clothes.

Just recently the deliberate loss of the centralized system of economic management was interpreted as a historical success, as a strategic breakthrough in our world view. But now, when so much has been unjustifiably butchered, an attempt is being made to backpedal.

It must be noted that some of our ultra-left (regarding the economy) politicians are literally beginning to become human. While they were government servants they appeared to be, behind the powerful covering from above, soulless technocrats and narrowly specialized robots, who were not familiar with the concept of social pain. Yet now, in pursuit of voters for their miniature parties, they carry on about the suffering of the people and about the economy, although, for instance, the former Minister of Finances did everything to weaken it and rejoiced every time it dropped by a percentage point, because he believed that otherwise reforms would not work.

The dominant mark of all decrees is the demand to bring fundamental discipline to the economy. For instance, each company has to have only one current and one budget account, and every quarter they must inform tax organizations about all their accounts both in the country and abroad. And, in case of ruble shortages, they must sell their currency and pay with the rubles they receive. To be fair, I must say that according to the old rules, companies had to have only one expense current account. As a result, the decree's requirement that companies could maintain one checking account was redundant, like beating a dead horse.

The long-lasting liberal game the government has been playing with companies has cost society a great deal. Tens of billions of dollars were taken abroad and there is no hope of seeing them return. How can it be possible not to heed the call heard in the decrees to return to common sense? The closer we move to a market economy, the more we have a need for good common sense. But the path we had chosen turned out to be hard to follow. This same decree (No.1005) has a number of positive items, but it suffers from administrative overkill. Now companies are obligated to pay bills in the order that the bank receives them. Freedom was replaced with a detailed regulation of activities. We are lucky that the president of a company is not ordered to come to work in a striped suit. However, in 1995, a new order appeared that salaries must be paid first, then the budget payments were to be paid, etc. This rule did not last. Due to the dismal state of the budget, the government made budget payments a priority in the second half of the year.

The President's initiative to lower taxes, which reduced basic taxes by 10%-20%, allowed entrepreneurs to breath a sigh of relief. But at the same time it was proposed to raise personal and property taxes. We can assume that the goal is to increase taxes on the rich. It is hard to argue against that. What if, against common sense, the tax increase is meant to affect those with an average income? After all, there can be no guarantee against bureaucratic recklessness. I can not hide yet another concern. It seems only natural that the overall tax increase should include property and profit (it is not even mentioned in the decree) taxes. But it is entirely possible that the organizations, eager to collect, will consider privatized apartments to be private property and will inflate taxes to the bursting point. Ordinary people have no other property. Thus, a Western tax policy, because of the rapacious nature of our authorities, may lead to further destructive bleeding of Russian society.

The decree on the reform of state enterprises was dictated by open discrimination toward state enterprises. When one starts settling personal accounts, everything suffers. Who can explain why it is necessary to outlaw the creation of self-supporting state enterprises? But if tomorrow we need to develop rapidly in some aspect of industry or technology and we find that private enterprises lack resources, we will be forced to use this outlawed method. The fact that state factories in Czarist Russia were in the vanguard of technical progress serves as a historical mockery of this decree. And now our state factories have been deprived of all rights. This condition is manifested in the form of fines for real or imaginary negligence and for breaking existing regulations. Several separate measures are considered to be violations, for instance, leasing property to other legal entities.

Why is a lease considered to be a harmful act? Under certain circumstances leases can be mutually beneficial. But perhaps the author of the decree (the President becomes the sole author once the decree is signed) thinks that by destroying the government sector and by absorbing some of the state enterprises into budgetary expenses, he is increasing the efficiency of productive forces? Decree #1003 requires that privatized state enterprises employ the same amount of workers employed at the time of privatization. This is hardly economically expedient. It could very well be that the lack of profit during the past two years is a result of over-employment, irrational working schedules, and concealed unemployment—all of which are reason to hand these enterprises over to the state. Instead of taking advantage of reforms and improving situations for new enterprises, Yeltsin is loading them down with the same weights. The new state enterprises would naturally have to renew their production program and orientation. Consequently, if a new state enterprise, for example, needs fitters, not turners, the director would still have to hire the turners who were laid off from a closed factory because the decree states that nobody has the right to refuse employment to former workers of a closed state factory. This reflects a concern for the possible emergence of unemployment, but it does not solve the problem. Unemployment is present in a latent state, regardless of the illusion of even minute success. Employment should be increased through retraining and job creation, as well as the new establishment of new private and state enterprises, but the latter is no longer permitted. And, at this point, expanding private entrepreneurship is extremely difficult.

The cancellation of quotas and export licenses will lead to complex and controversial consequences. A small number of manufacturers and resellers will no doubt get a lot of foreign currency as a result of this unprecedented foreign trade liberalism. But this will leave the domestic market destitute. After all, everybody knows that it is more profitable to sell for foreign currency than for rubles. The decree shows signs of the reformers' old dementia that leads to the belief that a smooth entrance into the world market will cure the domestic economy. A dog's coat is shiny when it is healthy. The first and foremost task of the upper administration is to create an internal interrelated domestic market based on market principles within the domestic economy. The attempt to revolutionize the collapsed national economy by integrating it into the world economy is a mistake and causes more harm than good. As a result, we will only increase the imbalance in the export of raw materials, which is already troublesome, given the astronomical prices for natural resources at home.

If one would have to define the term 'market economy' in one phrase it would be as follows: market economy is economic war with rules. The sides in this war are represented by companies that have no choice but to win or lose. I will add two more adjectives to this definition. First of all, this war is constant. It does not end in peace and general tranquillity. In the best case there can be a truce, which is by nature temporary. In the second place, this war is global. It necessarily involves all countries. Consequently, not a single national company can feel secure, even if it dominates the local market. The global market can blow up in its face, like a incoming missile shot from any corner of the globe.

What economic war with rules can we talk about if the Russian economy has been crippled? It has fallen into tenth place in regards to gross national product, and into seventieth place (1993) in terms of economic productivity. Moreover, according to 1995 statistics, it has continued to decline.

At one point in time I was able to publish an article on the Western shadow economy. The censors resisted publishing the article because it showed that the capitalist countries had greater potential than the socialist coalition. This meant that there was a larger discrepancy in the GNP per capita. I believe that underground activities make up 10% of an economy. For example, America's 'shadow' economy is equal in size to the entire Canadian economy. The omission of the 'shadow' economy from official statistical data distorts reality.

The problem of shadow economies in the West has not been resolved. The brightest minds argue about how to solve this problem. There are two extreme points of view. The first is to prohibit, to patrol, and punish. The counter-argument states that although such actions may lead to the decrease in underground business (there are dozens of synonyms for the term 'shadow' economy), many people may lose their jobs and this will exacerbate social problems. The second point of view is to allow everything, and as a result of this freedom, the economy will rise like dough and everybody will get a bigger piece of the pie. Opponents argue that this will inevitably lead to the collapse of social values and eventually to economic decline. It would behoove us to study how the West deals with this 'second' economy. But so far we have not done so.

There is no doubt that Yeltsin would like to abolish our illegal economy completely, but eliminating quotas and export licenses opens the doors to both honest and dishonest exporters. And in this exporting euphoria many honest people may become dishonest. How can one resist such temptation? Currency control has not yet been established. Nobody is in a hurry to declare how much money they have in foreign accounts as required by decree No.1006. And foreign banks, grateful for the business, have no intentions of divulging information about their clients. So the money will continue to drain into a black hole. The problem is even likely to worsen. By fighting lawbreakers, the government is relying on the violators having a conscience. This is typical Vasquesianism.

Let us take another example of Yeltsin inadvertently promoting a shadow economy. The President has implemented draconian measures against using large amounts of money. In reality, contracts are frequently paid with black market cash. These sums are not accounted for and they are not taxed. One does not need to study method acting to be able to imagine yourself in the entrepreneurs' role. Payments take days, weeks, or even months, and sometimes, in some CIS countries, they never arrive. What are business people to do—lose the deal and go under or break the law? What is the local administration to do if they want to supply the local stores with goods? Here is an example. A floating storage unit is situated off-shore with fresh fish, while at the seaport refrigerators stand empty and small wholesalers cannot legally buy the fish for cash. A long time may pass before the payment documentation gets through. Entrepreneurs frequently risk their money and their lives, setting out with suitcases full of money to pay the suppliers. If businessmen, who make up the President's support base, were to comply with decree No.1600 prohibiting cash payment, then a large number of them would be ruined. It is more likely that transactions will only become more secretive and officials will be bribed. Russia's salvation lies in ignoring destructive decrees.

Many radical reformers dream of mass economic bankruptcy. Only when this occurs, they say, will the long awaited for healing of the economy begin. Once radical reformers waited just as eagerly for domestic prices to rise to world market levels in the hopes that as soon as the prices evened out, the mechanism of global competition would kick in, spawning an economic miracle. But what happened? The prices on certain goods first reached and then exceeded world market levels, and there is no improvement in sight. A single sober look is sufficient to demonstrate that the bankruptcy being forced on us will only intensify the economic and social problems we face. Of course, unnecessary enterprises should be abolished, but the list of such enterprises should be compiled very carefully. We should not focus on closing existing enterprises, but rather on opening new ones. We should promote new businesses. They are the ones, along with existing companies, who will create a heretofore unprecedented competitive economic atmosphere. They will bring some rationality to the economy. In the meantime, nothing has really been achieved in this area, except for the creation of a stack of papers. The bureaucrats live by these papers. They defend themselves from just criticism by a time-tested method: of declaring that they have a program, a mandate and money.

Taking into consideration the destructive tendencies of the ruling elite, the preamble to Decree No. 1114 ("On the Selling of Government Enterprises in Debt") is a pleasant surprise in its announcement of a policy directed at combating the insolvency of enterprises. Objectively determining and carefully dissolving truly unnecessary enterprises is a necessity of our time.

Having just said something positive about the preamble, however, I am once again forced to return to my sad deliberations. Let us take, for example, Article 4 of this decree: if a government enterprise becomes insolvent for reasons not related to late payments from the federal budget or the budget of a subject of the Russian Federation, then the manager of the enterprise is responsible for the insolvency and is viewed as being unfit for the position.

But how do we evaluate those enterprises that are

insolvent because they did not receive payments from those who were deceived by the government? There is an indirect connection here. Moscow has played an ugly role by not paying farmers for the harvest to this day. The decree forgives the wheat growers, but it hounds the cooperating plants and others, linked together in this economic chain. There is a pathological hatred of directors of state enterprises, which is shared by many high-ranking bureaucrats.

There are other causes of insolvency that are on the government's conscience and should be mentioned here: the absence of long-term credits, an intolerably high interest rate on short-term loans, price monopolies, the canceling of business contracts, and still many others. But it turns out that the director has to answer for all this before the enterprise does. While the president is clear on the insolvency issue, the Prime Minister is not, even though he approved it. Two weeks before the decree came out (on May 16, 1994) he ordered the creation of a committee to determine the reasons for the insolvency of enterprises and of working out practical ways to eradicate insolvency in two months. This problem has been tormenting the country for years, and the main economist, who kept remarking "we have to work", finally decided to figure it out. What if this committee comes to the conclusion that the "red directors" are not to blame for everything. What then? Change the decree. We are used to that too. A decision that cannot be changed is indeed nefarious.

The second (June) packet of presidential economic measures opens with three decrees on housing. These steps can effect significant changes on the real estate market. During the Soviet era the state tried to provide housing for everyone but it was unable to successfully fulfill its task. Those who travel through Russia can see that brick cottages are mushrooming everywhere, predominantly outside of city limits. It is clear who owns these 'mansions.' These people are in a position to procure housing without the help of decrees. It is a different matter when it comes to the middle class, for whom the presidential actions create a glimmer of hope that they might obtain four walls to call their own. After food and clothing, housing is the most vital necessity, one which families are prepared to work and save for years. Among our economists the following sentence has become a widespread truth: just as the automobile evolving America, so private housing will change Russia. This is not entirely true, since private houses were just as significant in evolving America as was the automobile.

The construction of private houses contains a huge potential for starting our economy on a new footing. But we cannot be blinded to the factors that could jeopardize this housing boom. A principal danger is the uncertainty regarding private property, which is difficult to use under existing conditions as collateral for credit. I remember after disbanding the Congress of Peoples' Deputies, Yeltsin made an extremely important decision about land, which nonetheless has gone unrealized to this day. The new Parliament has yet to express its opinion on this matter yet. Signing the new decree (on housing credits), Yeltsin must understand that these credits cannot exist without land mortgages. If he does understand this, then we have to do with a case of demagoguery; if he does not, then it is just another case of bungling.

Decree No.1200 is entitled "On Some Actions To Assure Government Management of the Economy." The pro-market frenzy of the President has quieted down, and he is now forced to use the phrase that he so recently despised: "The government management of the economy." There is nothing new in this document. It implements practices that have been accepted worldwide, such as the that of signing contracts with supervisors of state enterprises and that of appointing government representatives to management positions in private corporations. If any funds are in the full or partial possession of the government, then it needs to manage them. In the West every student knows this, but the current administration resisted until the last minute when it found itself back at square one.

When I was Governor of Sakhalin, I insisted on forming a company to finish building an enormous structure that originally had been slated to house administrative offices. The construction had been going on for over ten years, but now was practically at a stand still. The whole project was in such a hopeless state that it seemed that no force—whether it be communism or fascism—could make things budge. The newly organized company completed construction of the monumental building in two years. It was re-profiled and became a business center and now plays an important role in supporting a business atmosphere on the island. The province owned half of the shares according to the charter, so I appointed my assistant to take part in the work of the company (without compensation naturally). Local snitches saw this as terrible corruption (the merger of government and business) and before long a police raiding group was sent in from Moscow to put an end to the Governor's tyranny and to arrest the Vice Governor. But those police officials turned out to be normal people. After we explained the situation they flew back. But the barrage of threats from Moscow had not ended, and at the Congress of People's Deputies no less than the Attorney General of Russia spoke of the blatant corruption uncovered on the island. Since I considered myself to be in the right, I implemented the same practice at other enterprises.

Now they have come to their senses and they are establishing an institute for the preservation of government interests on a federal level. But why only on a federal level? What about, for example, regional and other enterprises in which the government holds shares? Item No. 10 of Decree No. 1200 suggests that the executive bodies of the Federation should apply new rules when signing contracts with the supervisors of state enterprises. But there is not a single word about representing the interests of the subjects of the Russian Federation and lower-level. It is as though they simply forgot.

President Truman, it is said, used to make a pun about not being able to find any one-handed economists. Truman was fortunate in that his approach to life was simple. His economic advisors had a tendency to give him contradictory advice (in contrast to our straightforward marketers), first presenting arguments on the one hand, and then on the other hand. In the decree on the improvement of the banking system (No. 1184), paragraph six describes the work of foreign banks in Russia and Russian banks abroad. This passage is laden with unpredictable consequences. On the one hand, allowing foreigners to have access to our financial-credit system is desirable, since the development of competition is desired in all branches of the economy, although on a strictly limited basis. Their presence is needed more as an example than for actual competition, as the competition among Russian banks is quite stiff. They have even started to weed out and exhibit small-time operations—an incomprehensible act that smacks of a pathological attraction to everything big. If you are big enough - you can live, if you are small - die or be born as a one-year-old. What really should worry us here is the declared principle of 'an eye for an eye'—we will let your banks in if you do the same for ours. At this point the present approach is doubly unsuitable, since it will lead to money being siphoned abroad and to an increase in foreign debt. We have lit the candle at both ends, and it is burning fast.

Since Russia's debt has exceeded all acceptable limits, the President should decree a moratorium on new currency credits. The enormous amounts of wasted money did not help to overcome internal problems. On the contrary, they exacerbated them. A federal law that took effect on June 17, 1994, states that the maximum amount that the government can borrow from abroad in 1994 is 4.7 billion dollars, and Russia can give 400 billion dollars of foreign credit. Still, 4.7 billion dollars is too much. We also continued the practice of borrowing vast amounts of money from abroad in 1995, as well.

Asking for new foreign credits and then asking for an extension on the deadline for their repayment puts Russia in a humiliating position. The mechanism for the return of foreign debt has not been thought through and fails to take the real economic situation into account. The country does not need help from the West, the government does. They convert the sum according to a nonexistent exchange rate and then add the sum to the budget under the revenue. Logically, paying back hard currency debts will increase the debit column in the budget, but there is no money to pay when the debt is carried over (after us, the flood). So the actual budget deficit, taking into account the postponed payments, is far higher as a percentage of the GNP than is being presented to the people.

However, we cannot refuse to work with the West to resolve the problem of Russia's international debt. The process involves tying together and balancing out Russia's debit and credit loans in the world economy. The former socialist countries and developing nations owe Russia. With the end of the hostility between the two systems, western countries should show their good will and foster progressive changes in a number of countries rather than profiting from their troubles. The Russian State or the President should take the initiative in organizing such interaction.

Relying on foreign countries was and remains a mistake on the part of the Russian leadership. Instead of increasing domestic production levels and creating opportunities for domestic entrepreneurs, the government is doing what seems easier and clearer—relying on the rest of the world instead of on themselves. The global market is a big boxing ring where everyone fights for himself. You will not be beaten to death there, but neither will you be spared. We know of theories of the inequality of races and nations. Well, the global market creates a de facto inequality of national economies: the strong rule over the weak. To chase Russia from the upper levels to the basement is a disgrace for Russians and that is precisely what is happening with the help of the White House on Krasnopresnenskaya Street.

In addition, thanks to our reformers, the word of the leader of our country does not mean much in the international sphere. This is unprecedented. Whatever your attitude toward the USSR and its leaders, it is impossible to imagine Stalin, Khruschev or Brezhnev sitting in the waiting room of the "Big Seven."

The time has come for the government to deal with the exchange rate of the ruble, but, without a decree from the President, they will never block Russia's voluntary contributions to the world market. According to the calculations of the Russian Union of Industrialists and Entrepreneurs, and its buying power the ruble is significantly undervalued in comparison to the dollar. The calculations were made by the same methods used by the experts at the Foundation of Economic Cooperation and Development (FECD). Incidentally, if someone is surprised by the seemingly low value of the dollar, we can refer them to the research team of the British magazine, "The Economist," which determined the buying power of the dollar at approximately the same rate. The same magazine, explaining its calculations, called the ruble one of the most unjustly undervalued currencies of the world.

The regulation of the exchange rate of the ruble should be based on its buying power against the gross national product. If it is based on actual prices, it will fluctuate monthly depending on the structural changes in the GNP and in price changes. This revised rate would reflect the actual level of the national economic potential and must be used in all import-export transactions and in all other cases where the undervalued rate of the ruble, as determined by the Moscow Interbank currency exchange, is used. Thus, two exchange rates for the ruble must exist side by side, and the market rate must be used for a limited amount of transactions, for instance when individuals wish to purchase dollars for non-commercial purposes, by speculators of all types, etc.

The currency ceiling that was established by the government in June of 1995 (4300-4900 rubles to a dollar, and latter 4500-5150 rubles) is a step in the right direction, but it comes to late. A couple of years ago we were told that the abandonment of the floating rate was impossible and would be the equivalent of abandoning reform. Those who supported regulation of the exchange rate were accused of all sorts of things. Now all of a sudden, the government itself is implementing an anti-market policy that it justifies with arguments with which it used to disagree. So it is theoretically possible that tomorrow the government's position will change completely and again in the future.

Tacitus noted in his time that the most laws were written in times of trouble. We are now living in times of trouble and there is an abundance of quasi-laws, (i.e. decrees). This is because the State Duma and the government are not doing their job. The Duma, like a tank, has maneuverability. It pretends to be concerned with governing, while on the inside it is being torn apart by party and personal ambitions. We cannot blame it, just as you cannot blame a child for childish behavior. Many years must pass before democratic and parliamentary traditions will be established, and the deputies will acquire a sense of shame. It is even a good thing that the Duma is passive and, in keeping with the times, consumed by destructive feuds, because when a defective mechanism works of full force, nothing good can be expected of it.

As for the government, it is following the current, paddling lazily. Chernomyrdin is leaving everything to chance. Everyone is afraid to contradict the President for fear of being forced into retirement. The ministers follow suit. First they sign things and then they improvise. Before our very eyes the Ministry of the Economy is being dealt its final blow in the process started by Yeltsin. And nobody, least of all the Minister of the Economy, dares to interfere. He, like all members of the government, would like to stay on top for as long as possible. It is not in vogue to think of the Motherland. Those in power are democrats, not patriots, (i.e. one-legged invalids). The Ministry of the Economy is sharing the fate of the country's economy itself. A time will come when real politicians will have to restore the economy and the Ministry. The childishness of the Duma, along with the lack of independence of the cabinet, forced the President to act alone and again take all responsibility for the state of economic affairs that he at one point shunned, having named himself as the head of the government in his altered version of the constitution. Since in the same constitution he completely subordinated the government to himself, the President acts de facto as the main executive power, as well. There were plans to adopt the French system of government control, but in reality we surpassed the American system in terms of executive privilege. So ruling by decree is to be our destiny for a long time.

The Germans have a saying about a cow on ice. Our economy is in the same position. The decrees will not help it much. They contain a number of proper and necessary measures that have come too late. But at the same time these documents set in motion many undesirable processes in various spheres of the economy. Some of these have been listed above.

The new leadership, beginning in 1990, learned to

do one thing—to give off an artificial and cloying optimism in any situation. They continue to do so even today. Inflation, they say, has been lowered to an unprecedented level and the production rate will go up at any minute. Note that they are predicting that the United States economy will boom. Some of their professors honestly admit that they do not know the exact reasons for this phenomena. Evidently, the cyclical nature of production (which was the cause of Bush's down fall several years ago) comes into play here. But our specialists know it all, and they can already make out the light at the end of the tunnel. Unfortunately, the worst for our economy is yet to come. The lowering of inflation rates was achieved at enormous expense: the collapse of production. Sooner or later the government will be forced to take a different course of action—to support production.

Despite all the difficulties related to rebuilding the economy on a market basis, we should not over-dramatize the situation. It was far more difficult to build a planned economy in the first place. It took savage reprisals against those who would not agree to turn society upside down and to topple the economy, (i.e. to do everything contrary to the policies adopted by other civilized countries). It was more difficult for Stalin than for Yeltsin.

Under different leadership, we will finally arrive at a strong social economy—not through foreign financing, but through domestic production; not by destroying the government, but by achieving a reasonable balance of interests between it and society; and, finally and most obviously, through strong leadership.

We must not lose this war—the defeat of democracy in 1917 teaches us that lesson. We will once again return to 'tank socialism' if we give up now. But, I repeat, we cannot win the war by destroying the economy.

Chechnya

Columns of tanks have been sent to Chechnya
Crimson clouds are awaft
Will the mountaineer's sword penetrate the armor
That protects the troops
Or will it cause but a scratch?
The earth is shaking with fury
Descendants of Shamil will rise
Heeding their lands sacred call
The Caucasus will be consumed by flames of enmity
We learned not from the war of Czars

December 11, 1994
The day the Russian troops moved into Chechnya
to topple Dzhokhar Dudayev's regime.

"Caucasus surrender, Yermolov is coming,"-wrote
Pushkin. The locals used to scare their children with Yermolov's name. We should remember that.
They do in the Caucasus. An old friend of mine, a
Daghestani, thinks that the conquest of the Caucasus
brought Russia nothing but trouble and expenses
unlike, for instance, Siberia, whose resources support
the entire country. We must not forget, however, that
the Caucuses did contribute Stalin, Beria, and the Soviet
general Dudayev to the common cause.

The events in Chechnya hammered home two lessons that should inspire us to act accordingly.

Lesson number one: During difficult times Russia cannot rely on its democrats, such as Gaidar, Yavlinsky, Yushenkov, and Kovalyov. We are not talking about the personal qualities of these figures or about their nationalities. They could be pleasant to talk to and they might consider themselves loyal to Russia. But, it cannot be denied, they are causing great harm to Russia. Once we get to the essence of the issue, it is hard to stop asking the strange, surrealistic question: in what country and at what era are these people living? They see problems and daily concerns from outer space and from some future point in time when there will be no ethnographic borders and the entire world will be filled with goodness and happiness.

This is not an individual or chance pathology among Russia's democrats. It is a way of thinking. Consequently, it is impossible to try to convince them of anything. Their militant demagoguery must be overcome by an onslaught from the patriotic flank. Not only do the democrats proclaim that all people of all countries are brothers and sisters, they actually make an effort to realize their ideas. Yet their efforts are one-sided, and they are at Russia's expense. They do not regret that the USSR collapsed and refuse to learn from their mistakes. Even if you think that the Soviet Union was an evil empire (As did Reagan- Yeltsin, to some extent, shares his opinion), Russia should not be subjected to such torment. The fact that different countries have different interests in the world, seems to be beyond the understanding of the democrats. Yet foreign leaders, such as Bush, Thatcher (before whom Yeltsin, as he himself admits, bows,) Mitterand, and others, have always defended the interests of their own nations. We should at least be playing the same game as they are.

These interests coincide in some ways (this could easily be seen as the brotherhood mentioned earlier). But frequently they do not coincide but rather brutally collide. Rancor arises as the result of economic disagreements and territorial issues (the Falkland islands, Gibralter) among other things. There is a constant tug of war in the international arena that demands the use of all government's resources. Our democrats think that there is no such tug of war. They attack their own side. The democrats' constant demand for the resignation of those close to Yeltsin is revealing. Not once did they demand Dudayev's resignation. That is to say they joined ranks with Dudayev, who himself did not have the time to award them with medals for their achievements in the fight against Russia. Although I must admit that Dudayev turned out to be not as ordinary as his enemies portrayed him to be, he was able to make his personal conflict with the Kremlin into a struggle for the independence of the Chechen nation.

The determination of the rebels in this struggle merits respect. We actually should not have expected anything less. If we found ourselves in a similar situation in Mother Russia, we would fight with the same fervor to defend its altars and hearths.

In their attempts to set international opinion against Russia, our democrats are not ashamed to use any means. They argue that the war in Chechnya will inevitably lead to the end of reform in Russia, although these things are not related. Their anti-Russian feelings are also betrayed by their call to organize a one-sided Nuremberg trial for the instigators of the Chechen war. We need to be ready for everything — from a five star hotel abroad to prison in our own country.

Lesson number two: The ineptitude of the current Russian leadership is creating unnecessary internal and international problems of a serious nature. Yeltsin's argument about Chechnya is basically as follows. We waited for three years and thought that the situation would improve, but Dudaev mistook our peaceful disposition for weakness. As a result Chechnya became the bastion of criminal forces. We were forced to act. Everything about the President's argument is wrong. Why did he wait for three years if an anti-Constitutional coup had taken place in one of the parts of the Russian Federation? Out of pride Yeltsin will not admit that he would have dealt with Grozny a long time ago if the Supreme Soviet of the Russian Federation had let him, but at the time he was not a sovereign president. For over a year after the Supreme Soviet was dissolved in the fall of 1993 and after the December elections (1993) he was in a position to seriously deal with Chechnya but he did not want to. He was waiting. What was he waiting for? He was just waiting. This is our President's favorite tactic. There is once again a hidden reason for his behavior. After the new Constitution was enacted (December 1993) he assumed a new position. He was organizing the government and proving himself. Having bolstered his position at the flanks, he decided to raise his rating with an instantaneous victory over Dudayev. It did not work. You can never be sure which hook will catch a fish and which hook you might get caught on. Let us be extremely lenient and forgive Yeltsin his three idle years. But now we shall ask without mercy, "couldn't he have at least used those three years to prepare for the invasion?" It was here that his feeble mindedness became evident. It had been hidden behind his inaction. One cannot, however, conceal feeble-mindedness when taking decisive action. Have we forgotten the triumphant surgical strike that Washington launched against Noriega's regime in Panama. The dictator was arrested, delivered to the USA, and tried on narcotics and other charges. Now he is in prison and nobody condemns the USA. What about the landing of the American troops in Haiti, when they deposed the coup-plotting general, and later reinstated the popularly elected President Aristide, who was brought back from the USA. It is said that Aristide is not of sound mind. Once again the world did not protest. On the contrary the action was met with approval. Everybody still remembers "Desert Storm"—Bush's venture into far away lands against Saddam Hussein.

When the columns of tanks entered Chechnya by Yeltsin's order ("nothing happens in Chechnya without me") on December 11, 1994, the USA supported this act, expecting that the events would be directed in a civilized fashion. The necessity of the governments intervention was not questioned, as the unlawful separation threatened the territorial integrity of the state— the holiest of holies in classical politics. The French term coup d'etat needs no translation and is known world wide. Both the observers and the participants of the operation assumed that all details were thought through. But instead of a sprint it turned into a marathon of carnage that changed popular opinion and turned it against Russia and, within Russia itself— against the government.

Those are the two lessons. As we noted, studies on economies abroad recommend that businesses draw on military experience to help them succeed. This would be unwise in our country. Our military actions are just as half-witted as our economic policies. It could be no other way—the cast of characters is the same. Instead of the instant change to a market economy predicted by Yeltsin at the end of 1991 and beginning of 1992, the country got a huge and prolonged crisis. There was really no chance for a rapid transition. But as Nekrasov wrote, once you are seized by a whim you can't beat it out with a crowbar. Although he had the Russian peasant in mind, the same saying goes for the Czars, both past and present. On a whim the inherited economic system is being destroyed before and simultaneously through the construction of an alternative (market) economy. And when it became necessary to have a lightening round between the two Presidents (Yeltsin and Dudayev), with no chance that either could win, the result was the systematic annihilation of the Chechen capital, cities, villages and the bombing of Russia's own population—after all Moscow does not acknowledge the sovereignty of Chechnya. I brought up the economy in order to call attention to Mammon, the god of economy in ancient Eastern mythology, who with eyes turned towards Russia stands bitterly crying . When he manages to keep from crying he makes an expressive gesture by twirling his index finger around his temple.

The era of democratic changes in today's Russia has been marked with the blossoming of new lies, in contrast to the old ones told by Stalin and Brezhnev. These lies were necessary to camouflage the fiascoes caused by those in power. In regard to Chechnya, the democrats used a primitive lie (the brain washing carried out by Goebbels and the Bolsheviks was much more refined), despite the fact that telling the whole truth about Dudayev's regime would have been more beneficial to Yeltsin. Yet in failing to precede the military action with an educational campaign, Moscow revealed that it had forgotten the fundamentals of propaganda. Only later did Russian politicians began disseminating information about the thousands who perished in Chechnya over the previous three years. And, Shakhrai, the leading specialist on Chechnya—as well as all other issues of nationality policies, promised to tell the world other chilling details of their master plan (for example, about plans to attack an atomic power plant). All of the governments actions smacked of improvisation and the patching of holes that were obvious to all.

When Avturkhanov (he is already forgotten) was dethroned in the Nadterech region, Yeltsin was asked to what degree Moscow would intervene. Yeltsin, making his typical hand gesture, answered that Moscow was helping Avturkhanov, but not very much, because if he were to offer full scale military support the war might spread across the entire Caucasus. This "not very much" lasted a few months. In October of 1994 Avturkhanov's tanks rolled into the square right up to Dudayev's palace but he was defeated because Russia did not really support him due to its fears of starting a war in the Caucasus. In November when the exact same thing was repeated, even this last golden opportunity was missed.

Grachev denied any Russian participation. He pretended not to recognize Russian planes that the world saw daily over Grozny. "Those are not our planes and that's all there is to it," he insisted, evidently not understanding, that he was striking a fatal blow to his reputation. If planes take off in Russia and the leaders know nothing about it, then everyone with a high rank on their shoulders should retire—maybe to Siberia or prison. Remember the incident involving Rust, who landed his plane in Sheremetyevo-3, as someone cleverly called the landing spot near Red Square. Many generals suffered as a result. The Minister of Defense, Sokolov, was also fired. Rust himself was punished. Grachev did not recognize his own soldiers, who had been taken prisoners either. Once, posing as superman, Grachev proclaimed that with one regiment of paratroopers he could defeat Dudayev in but two hours.

The Minister's bravado helped lead to Yeltsin's change of position, as he took the Minister's words at face value. So he did not let the Chechen's settle things among themselves, and he did not help Avturkhanov out of the fear that a war would break out. As a result he let himself get sucked into a real war of the worst kind and was forced into a fight to the finish. Because if Russia is defeated, she will be ordered about by anybody and everybody from its own national republics to foreign states. Although according to Brzezinski, Russia is no longer the USA's partner but a beggar with the standard of living of an African nation. And what about Grachev? He continued to demolish Chechen territory, drawing on his experience in Afghanistan.

As far as imagination goes, the Minister is the equal of the great writer who wrote a story about an officer's widow who flogged herself. According to one circulated version of events, the Chechens were involved in bombing themselves.

It is well known that a lie has short legs and a long tail. You cannot hide it under a camouflage uniform. Let us take a close look at some public announcements made by the commander of the Air Force:

ï   "We are strictly adhering to president Yeltsin's decree and are not bombing
Grozny."

ï   "We are not bombing Grozny, but the military installations in Grozny."

ï   "Due to unfavorable weather conditions our precision military equipment may falter, consequently it is possible that we may hit non-military objects."

He said this all in one breath without noticing that he inadvertently admitted to bombing Grozny. It is no use talking about the intelligence of such generals.

They are just splashing about in puddles while dressed in their pretty uniforms. On some occasions, the Israeli General Moishe Dayan, a wonderful strategist from the not so distant past, is portrayed in conversation by covering one eye with a palm. (Dayan lost one eye during a military operation.) To convey what the generals who are conducting operations in Chechnia are like, you would have to cover both eyes and nod your head back and forth.

But the behavior of some other aides and assistants to the President leaves you with a feeling of distaste. Deep down they disagree with their boss's decision, but they are afraid to speak out honestly. They act like toadies and, in doing so, they hold on to their cushy jobs with their secretaries and direct lines to the President. From time immemorial we have been familiar with the image of the sly court intrigant. He will never die. He will always be needed by someone, in this case by Yeltsin, who uses him like a dishrag.

That's what our teacher said—with these words scholiasts referred to Aristotle as to the highest authority. That's what the boss said—the current bureaucrats refer to Yeltsin as the source of all benefits, as they make faces at him behind his back.

When Khruschev was removed from office in 1964, the President of France DeGaulle exclaimed—that's how glory passes. Chechnya signified the end of Yeltsin's glory in the West. And thank God. After all, in order to maintain that glory further, Yeltsin would have to repeat what he had done to the USSR of breaking Russia up into its national components, leaving only a scrap of the great nation—belts from the West to the East, all the way to the South Kuril Islands, which he will not, I hope, ever again even think about giving to Japan in order to become an honorary Japanese (a la Gorbachev, the honorary German). They both acted the part of Dudayev in regard to the Southern Kuriles. How can we forget the exclamation about the times and customs?

So, Yeltsin, wounded in both legs crawled into Chechnya. By his wounded legs I mean the inadequate military leadership and the useless propaganda. When it comes to current events, Yeltsin is very well informed. The statement that the President is unaware of what is going on—is gibberish coming from his gray-haired detractors. These boy-men (there is such a creature) are themselves ignorant of the fact that the president has a full set of facts. In 1991 at a meeting of the Presidential Council (at the time I was a member) the same question came up and Yeltsin dispelled all doubts, stating that he receives information from four different independent sources. The conclusions he makes based on this sea of information is another matter entirely.

Now what? I don't know who wanted to see the resolution of the Chechen issue take a tragic turn. It is unbearable to see the suffering of innocent people who are faced with death and destruction at the hands of both opposing sides. But the bloody deed has been done. There can be no higher price for victory in a region of that size. And here a question of cardinal importance arises: Can something similar happen again? It can. At any time another "horrible child" can appear.

If we go from this specific incident to a general conclusion, we find that we have rid ourselves of Bolshevism only partially. We got rid of the dictatorship of the party, but the national-territorial way of dividing the country that the party created in place of the former territorial principality remains unchanged. This is not normal. We cannot go on living on a powder keg of national separatism which creates a constant threat that Russia might blow up from within. In America there is only America. In Russia there has to be only Russia and the nations should live in free national cultural diversity.

According to the Constitution of the country, the name Russian Federation and Russia are different. We should review this item, which always leads to divisiveness. We should keep only one name—Russia. Once the Congress of the People's Deputies of the Russian Federation did just that, but the new name lasted only one day. The next day under the pressure of the autonomous regions, the Congress gave in and voted to give the terms Russia and Russian Federation equal status. Such a duality prohibits the establishment of equality between subjects, (i.e. between the provinces and regions on the one hand and the republics on the other). We know that Russia has 89 territorial subdivisions including 21 republics. By definition the republics and not the provinces [territories] and regions, compile the Russian Federation. Therefore they should have more rights. Why more and not less or the same as the indigenous Russian territories? In the Constitution all territorial subdivisions are considered to be equal, but in reality it is not so. Discrepancies between the Constitution and reality is nothing new to us. We lived for seventy years with a Constitution (or rather Constitutions) that on paper, was the most democratic, although the regime was clearly not the most democratic. Russia cannot be the vassal of its republics. Some regions increase their independence through attempts to eliminate inequalities. For instance, the Sverdlovsk Region pronounced itself the Ural Republic. Moscow, however, viewed this act as illegal and the governor was fired. The idea of creating a Far East republic is floating around. It is not such an abstract idea. Such a republic existed in the 1920s.

What am I getting at? Of course Moscow must decrease its control over the regions, but the regions, on their part must not threaten the unity of the country. Yeltsin already missed one chance to strengthen the country in this regard. Immediately after October 3-4, 1993, the White House, with its empty broken windows and smoke remaining from the fire, symbolized the end of Soviet power. Foreigners excitedly bought photographs of the damaged bastion of the Soviet system. Yeltsin did not realize at the time that he was dealing with a multi-headed hydra and that he only chopped off the first head. What's more, he even started feeding this hydra, by citing agreements between Moscow and the republics. Now he has managed to bite off another head, but the rest of them are biding their time. Yeltsin is a destroyer, not a builder. If Yeltsin did at one point sing "Guadeamus", then it was in vain. He has to make Russia into Russia and in order to do so he needs to implement territorial management by principalities.

During Yeltsin's term as President of Russia a lot of mistakes have been made in various areas. They were made both by the President himself and by those surrounding him. Some of these mistakes have been analyzed above.

But it must be stated just as firmly that these mistakes and miscalculations are not the only thing that has determined the changes that have occurred to date. We have been able to make sizable strides toward strengthening the democratic foundation of the country and toward creating a mixed economy.

Near the end of his first term as President, Yeltsin thought out and formulated his plan of action more fully. It became clear in what direction the country needed to move to further the interests of the people and the country. In the beginning a euphoria from destroying the old system prevailed. With it came an almost romantic belief that the market and general well-being would appear on their own, as soon as nongovernmental structures were allowed to exist freely. Now these illusions have almost completely disappeared. Also disappearing is the naive view of Western countries, who actually have no desire to help Russia, based on universal values. Under these circumstances it is very important to establish stable policies, that will guarantee the establishment of the conditions for Russia's rebirth.

I mean first of all:

*halt the lowering of the population's standard of living and start to raise it;

*declare war on crime;

*bolster the economy;

*in the international arena, guarantee Russia's security and solve the debt problem.

The government should be led in security in this direction by someone who understands what is required.

Now we are getting Russia on track and we must protect her from dangers, which include a number of ambitious politicians, who cannot resist their own desire to become ruler of Russia, leading to dire consequences for Russia herself.

About The Author

Valentin Fedorov was born September 6, 1939 in the city of Yakutsk. His childhood and early adolescence were spent on the banks of the Lena river, where he nearly drown three times.

He graduated from secondary school with honors. He became a student of the Plekhanov Institute of the National Economy in Moscow.

"Time changes the ratio of power, and the politician feels these changes like a mathematician feels his numbers. To miss opportunity - is simple, but to create opportunity, to influence circumstances requires effective political leaders." - says Fedorov.

His personal motto is "do the best you can, the rest is fate."

For two years after graduation from the Institute, Valentin worked as Chief Economist at the Yakutsk State Planning Committee. Already during that time he saw a picture of the primitive Soviet economy, without any future.

In 1964 he successfully passed entrance examinations for post graduate school at the Institute of World Economy and International Relations (IWEIR) at the USSR Academy of Sciences. Upon his graduation he wrote Candidate dissertation. In 1977 Valentin Fedorov completed his Doctoral dissertation on international affairs. Valentin spent a total of 21 years working for the Institute, including six years at the editorial office of the magazine World Economy and International Relations and six years in West Germany as the Institute representative.

During Fedorov's tenure at IWEIR he worked with the best world economic and political experts. He met successfully the challenge of intellectual and professional competition. In 1984 after Valentin returned form Germany he openly promoted market economy. These ideas led to a divergence of opinion between Fedorov and the institute management. Within a year he decided to leave the institute. He returned to his native Plekhanov Institute where he restarted work on his original studies of the Soviet Economy, in particular he recommended an economic experiment on Sakhalin Island, Russia.

Fedorov spent five years "fighting" for Sakhalin. In 1990 be became the People's Deputy representing Sakhalin Island after defeating 9 local candidates. Soon after that, at the Regional meeting of the Soviet People's Deputies he was elected Chairman of the Regional Executive Committee. He distinguished himself by working independently and acting decisively.

"Still in Moscow I thought through many times about Sakhalin", says Fedorov, - "I knew my time in Sakhalin would be limited, so I recognized that only the power of leadership offered a chance to implement a reform.

He was against transferring the Kuril Islands to Japan. In 1991 Fedorov accompanied Gorbachev to Japan. The Soviet President's willingness to give up the islands caused Valentin to publicly criticize the policy.

He addressed the problems of the Kuril Islands in his open letter to Boris Yeltsin. Through an article in the Sakhalin newspaper Gubernskye Vedomosti (9/12/92) he addressed A. I. Solzhenizhin with the request "to raise a voice to protect Russia's territorial integrity". The conclusion of this letter was "It's not enough to be a democrat, one has to be a patriot."

He was an authoritarian leader and openly ridiculed the ignorance and weakness of regional deputies-oppositionists. At the time he refused the ideas of the local extremists to start an economic struggle with the government. "One cannot start boxing with Moscow, instead one should play chess." He was absolutely against creating a Far East Republic.

In 1991 he presented to the Government a concept for existing the crisis known as "The 500-Week Program". The main idea of the program is the gradual (over a ten year period) transfer to the market economy observing the following conditions:

1. Creation of a parallel economic structure in the form of many new non-state enterprises as the main market economy condition (this principle is known as three F's: forms, firms, and

farms);

2. Careful dismantling of existing economic system by privatizing of enterprises and annual reduction of production per Governmental plan by 10%.

3. Orientation on the local not foreign means of development.

However, Gaidar's concept of the new reform was accepted. Fedorov called this reform "an unproven gamble".

Fedorov rejected twice an opportunity to become a member of the Supreme Soviet of Russia. He rejected an offer in 1991 to become a member of the Russian Government. Later he explained that the time had not come yet. "I need Sakhalin as an experimental ground, I haven't done everything yet."

Fedorov was a member of Yeltsin's Presidential Council. In 1993-1994 he was a Deputy Minister of Economics of Russia. From April 1994 to present he is a Vice President of the Russian Union of Industrialists and Entrepreneurs.

"I'm interested in performance, not excuses", - says the former Governor Fedorov.